VGM Opportunities Series

OPPORTUNITIES IN
FEDERAL GOVERNMENT CAREERS

Neale Baxter
Revised by
Mark Uri Toch

Foreword by
Constance Berry Newman
Director
United States Office of Personnel Management

VGM Career Horizons
a division of *NTC Publishing Group*
Lincolnwood, Illinois USA

Cover Photo Credits:
Front cover: upper left, USDA Forest Service;
upper right, The White House; lower left, VISTA;
lower right, USDA Forest Service.

Back cover; upper left, VISTA; upper right,
Bureau of Land Management, Department of the
Interior; lower left, USDA Forest Service;
lower right, U.S. Air Force.

Library of Congress Cataloging-in-Publication Data

Baxter, Neale.
   Opportunities in Federal government careers / Neale Baxter

      p.   cm. — (VGM opportunities series)
      Includes bibliographical references.
         1. Civil service positions—United States. I. Title.
   II. Series
   JK716.B38   1992
   353'.00023—dc20   91-43587
                                                    CIP

Published by VGM Career Horizons, a division of NTC Publishing Group.
© 1992 by NTC Publishing Group, 4255 West Touhy Avenue,
Lincolnwood (Chicago), Illinois 60646-1975 U.S.A.

2 3 4 5 6 7 8 9 0 VP 9 8 7 6 5 4 3 2 1

ABOUT THE AUTHOR

Neale Baxter is managing editor of the *Occupational Outlook Quarterly,* a general career information magazine published by the U.S. Department of Labor. He has also served with the U.S. Army overseas and worked for state and local governments. He has written for *Career World* and the *Monthly Labor Review,* and teaches at George Mason University.

Mr. Baxter received his Bachelor's degree from Manhattan College, his Master's from Purdue University, and his Ph.D. from the University of North Carolina at Chapel Hill. He resides in Virginia with his wife and two children.

ACKNOWLEDGMENTS

The editors gratefully acknowledge Mark Uri Toch for his assistance with this edition of the book.

FOREWORD

The federal government offers a career where one serves as the trustee of the people. Henry Clay made the following observation in May of 1829: "Government is a trust, and the officers of the government are trustees; and both the trust and the trustees are created for the benefit of the people."

Careers in the federal government are exciting and honorable because they offer an opportunity to make a difference in solving the problems facing the nation and the world. Public servants can make a difference in solving the problems of the homeless, the illiterate and the school dropouts. Public servants can protect our environment. . . from air pollution, from the pollution of drugs and from crime. Those who have chosen a career with the federal government can make a difference in Eastern Europe, in Africa, and in Latin America. Name any part of the world, America's public servants can make a difference.

In addition to providing an opportunity to make a diffence, the federal government should be considered as employer of first resort for two other reasons. First, a federal government career provides an opportunity for people to enter into meaningful positions right out of school and then move quickly into even more meaningful positions. Second, the federal government provides the kind of training and development opportunities that allow skills to be easily transferred from one challenging area to another.

Opportunities in Federal Government Careers is an excellent career guide. Generally I do not suggest that people begin their mysteries at the end. However, let me recommend your beginning with Chapter 12, "Three Government Workers—Why Some People Work For the Government." That will explain the attraction of the federal government. Once convinced you can then use the book as a road map for, among other things, the types of occupations, the federal agencies' descriptions, hiring procedures, salary and benefits.

Now more than ever in recent times the nation's leaders recognize the importance of public service. On January 26, 1989, President Bush said to a group of people who work for the federal government: "There is nothing more fulfilling than to serve our country and your fellow citizens and to do it well. And that's what our system of self government depends upon. And I've never known a finer group of people than those I have worked with in government. You're men and women of knowledge, ability and integrity. You work hard, you sacrifice, you deserve to be recognized, rewarded and certainly appreciated."

You should choose the federal government for your career. It would be an exciting, rewarding career where you can make a difference.

Constance Berry Newman
Director
United States Office of
Personnel Managment

CONTENTS

Additional (optional) training. Transfer privileges. Job security. Retirement.

A full career. Training pays off. Only in government.

Trying to solve unsolvable problems. Politics and promotion: an uneasy marriage. Lack of prestige and other drawbacks.

Visit. Books. Federal job information centers.

CHAPTER 1

FINDING A JOB WITH THE FEDERAL GOVERNMENT

Over three million civilians work for the federal government, making it far and away the largest single source of jobs in the country. If you want to work, ignoring the federal government is like wanting to buy a car and ignoring General Motors. Ignore the federal government and you ignore an employer who hires up to 1,000 people a day in jobs ranging from mail clerk to nuclear physicist, pays good starting salaries, offers fine training, and practically guarantees promotion through the middle ranks. Furthermore, for some kinds of work, such as engineering and law, it is the major employer in the country, while for others, such as law making, law enforcement, and air traffic control, the government is the only game in town.

Federal workers are employed in all parts of the United States and around the world. About 95 percent work in the United States and 5 percent in foreign countries. Although Washington, D.C., has the largest percentage of federal workers, only about 15 percent of the total work force is employed in the nation's capital.

If you want to land one of these government jobs, you will have to do more than send out a letter or two. Although the largest single employer, the federal government does not have only a single employment office. It has hundreds. No one person, no one office, no one agency can direct you to all the openings available at any given time—and, despite freezes, cutbacks, and hiring ceilings, some openings are being filled at every given time. No one book can give you all the answers, either; however, this one gives you a place to start.

1

This book describes the government's hiring procedures in a manner that helps you get yourself in a position to be among the people who can be hired. It explains how to describe your background in terms that will make a bureaucrat's antennae vibrate, so that you will be among the people considered for an opening. It tells you how to learn about the people who actually do the hiring, so you can find out where the openings are, and points you toward the largest agencies and occupations, so that your search can start where it is most likely to succeed. At the back of the book, there are even chapters on the pluses and minuses of government employment, explaining why some people work for for the government and why some people do not.

Although the 1980s was a time for cutbacks for many government programs, employment in the federal government did not decline to the same extent as employment at the state and local level. The last several years has seen a reorganization of hiring priorities for the U.S. government. What this has meant is not so much a reduction in the total number of federal workers, but a reduction in the growth of many agencies. While agencies like Labor and Health and Human Services saw a 25 percent reduction in personnel during the 1980s, agencies like the U.S. Postal Service and the Defense Department had sizable increases in the number of workers during this same period.

While it is difficult to predict future government hiring practices, it seems certain the government will continue to hire many thousands of people a year. The trick of course is to have the proper training and job approach to be one of those people.

CHAPTER 2

HIRING PROCEDURES

THE OFFICE OF PERSONNEL MANAGEMENT (OPM)

To talk about the government's hiring procedures is to talk about the *Office of Personnel Management,* and one of the first things to say about it is that it is a personnel office, not an employment agency. The Office of Personnel Management does not hire people, other than those who will actually work for that office. It makes the rules that govern the hiring practices of most government agencies and sees that the rules are followed.

You can look at hiring procedures in two ways: from across the desk of a person who needs a worker and from the sore feet of a person who needs a job. The view across the desk is the one taken by the Office of Personnel Management.

The role of the OPM has changed greatly in the last few years. Until the mid-1980s, OPM was the agency most responsible for hiring government employees. OPM recruited and screened most applicants, tested applicants, gave ratings, maintained registers of qualified applicants, and examined SF–171s. (The Standard Form 171, the government application form, is explained in greater detail in the next chapter.)

Although the OPM did not make final hiring decisions, it would provide a list of qualified candidates to the hiring agencies.

The hiring process is now much more decentralized. Individual agencies take the lead role in announcing vacancies and rating, interviewing, and selecting applicants. OPM provides overall support and ensures compliance with federal hiring practices, but prospective employees must now take a much more active role in contacting individual agencies to identify openings.

FEDERAL JOB INFORMATION CENTERS (FJIC)

FJICs operate as regional and local offices of OPM with the primary purpose of providing assistance to anyone looking for a federal job. FJICs provide full job announcements and application forms. In addition, these offices tell you where and how to apply for jobs and refer you to testing locations or employing agencies.

Although FJICs fill a vital role in providing job announcements and making the hiring process more accessible, there are some shortcomings to the system. Many of these centers do not have attendants, so all the information is posted on the wall. Interested applicants complete an address label noting the information they desire and put it into a mail slot. Several days later, the person will receive the desired job information and an application form. The FJIC phone numbers are also often of limited value. The phone lines often only offer prerecorded information or the phones are answered only during specified hours. For a complete listing of the FJICs, see chapter 14.

PRACTICE COURSES AND SAMPLE TESTS

Some profit-making schools offer civil service exam practice courses. Some people benefit from these courses, but before agreeing to take one, find out *exactly* what will be taught and exactly *how much* you will have to pay. Never take a course if the school tells you the government requires it or if the school says it can guarantee you a government job. Such statements are lies. *No course is required for any test.* In fact, none is even approved by the Office of Personnel Management. And no one can promise you a job.

Different written tests are given for different types of federal jobs. There is no single "Civil Service Test" that is given for all federal jobs. Also many types of jobs do not require a written test.

CHAPTER 3

A FORM TO FILL OUT—"THE 171"

For the want of a nail, says an old nursery rhyme, the war was lost. Similarly, for the want of a properly completed application form, your government job may be lost. Several forms are used, but the most common is *Standard Form 171*.

The Standard Form 171 (SF-171) is the personal qualifications statement of the federal government. It functions as the equivalent of a resume. Some people quip that it is called The 171 because it takes that many hours to finish. It doesn't really take that long to complete, but it will require a good piece of your time (perhaps several days). The time is well worth spending, however, because it is the single most important form you will fill out in your quest for a federal job.

The SF-171 is the first description of your qualifications that anyone will see. Fill it out carelessly, and it will be the last of you that they want to see. Put some work into it, type it neatly, and pack it with information, and it might get you an interview. Although not all federal agencies require the SF-171 (the Postal Service, for example, does not), most agencies will require it.

Obtain a copy of the form from the Federal Job Information Center (addresses are listed in chapter 14). As soon as you receive the form, photocopy it. Make several blank copies to use for drafts. Probably, you will even want more than one final draft or master copy. The SF-171 is a four-page application form.

The instructions are clear, in most cases, so you probably won't have any difficulty deciding what is supposed to go in the blanks. The rest of this chapter concerns the items that aren't self-explanatory.

5

You might expect the first item on the form to be an easy warm-up for the workout to come. It isn't. The first item is *"Kind of job you are applying for."* That sounds simple enough, but you will probably want to apply for more than one kind. You don't want to spend several hours each week typing out new SF-171s, because different agencies use slightly different job titles. So leave the first item blank on your master copy. Use the photocopies to apply for particular openings, filling in the job title and other variables, such as salary level, just before you send it off. Other than item 1, the first dozen blanks on the SF-171 don't raise any difficult questions.

Item 13 asks for the *lowest pay or grade that you will accept.* Pay rates change every year, so it's simpler to put down the grade. Besides, supervisors think of openings in terms of grades rather than salaries, so the grade means more to them. The grade systems are explained in Chapter 11, "Salary and Other Benefits."

Deciding which grade to put down is a dilemma. You may well be qualified for a higher grade than the position is for. Say you are a college graduate with two full years of relevant work experience; that combination qualifies you for a GS-9 salary in many occupations. But far more hiring goes on at the GS-7 and GS-5 levels. Demand a GS-9, and you will be screened out during the first run through the applications. On the other hand, put down GS-7 and you probably will not be hired as a GS-9, no matter how impressive you are at an interview. Leave this item blank on the master copies of your SF-171, so that you can fill in the appropriate level, depending on a specific announcement. You can even check with the office doing the hiring to learn if there is any chance of the position being filled at a higher level. You might even find out that an announcement was issued for the higher level, although you didn't come across it in your search. Still, for many occupations—engineer and secretary are major exceptions—you will probably have to accept a lower grade than your qualifications warrant. You will then have to decide if the position and the near certainty of promotion after a year is worth more than staying where you are.

Items 14 through 17 are fairly simple. They concern *things such as your willingness to travel, to work part-time, and to accept temporary appointments.* Officials have an easier time hiring someone who already has a federal job than they do when they hire from the outside. For this reason, accepting temporary or part-time positions often pays off. If you impress your supervisor, you may be offered a permanent position. If not, at least you will be more likely to learn of other jobs with the agency you work for than you would be if you were unemployed. On the other hand, the more hours you work, the less time you will have to job hunt.

Items 18 through 22 concern military service and veteran preference. If you've had military experience, or are the spouse, widow, or mother of a veteran, you can receive a 5 to 10 point advantage in your eligibility rating. (A large percentage of male federal employees are former veterans.) If you claim a veteran preference, you will have to supply documentation for this claim.

At this point on the form, you've completed almost half the items. Perhaps, you may say to yourself, this form is not the monster you had been told to fear. You turn the page. Your fears are realized. There crouches the beast: *Item 24—Experience.*

Item 24 makes you or breaks you. Anything you leave out will lower your chance for a job. Everything you put in raises it.

For every job you've held, starting with your current one and working backwards, you need to give the job's title, name and address of the employer, dates employed, and number of hours worked each week. You must also describe the work you did.

This is the item that will differ most in your various master copies. Let the announcements be your guide on how each can be slanted toward the position for which you are applying. Pay close attention to the language used in the qualifications statements and position descriptions. Then use similar words when you describe your own experience. Certain verbs occur again and again in the announcements, words like *coordinate, organize,* and *direct.* Use them. If the position announcement says, "Incumbent performs analytical and evaluative work," and you were a bookkeeper, write "Evaluated and analyzed financial material," instead of "Figured out and kept track of bills."

The announcement will include a section even more important than the description of work assignments and minimum qualification requirements. It is the "Evaluation Factors" that are given at the end of the announcement. The people who review your experience will do so in terms of these factors. If one factor is "ability to work independently," you must show that you have that ability. Don't trust the evaluators to figure out for themselves how well your experience matches the factors they are told to look for. Make the relationship explicit by using the same language as that used in the announcements.

The language in the announcements and qualifications statements is not very smooth—and sometimes is not even clear—but it is the language that hiring officials recognize. When you use it, be prepared to elaborate on what you did in the same terms at an interview. For example, if asked how you evaluated and analyzed financial material, you don't want to say, "Oh, I just kept track of the bills." You want to say something like, "When invoices and statements of charges were received, I reviewed them to ensure that they accurately reflected the charges agreed upon." Such a statement may sound awkward, but it is a truthful description of your duties.

A bare, bald statement of your duties isn't necessarily an accurate description of your experience. Add exact figures and concrete examples whenever possible. For example, don't write "Checked applications for completeness." Your SF-171 will have much more punch if you put, "Checked seven different kinds of insurance applications for completeness; forms were six to twelve pages in length." Such a statement gives your potential employer a much clearer idea of the work you did.

Make your descriptions as complete and exact as possible. At the very least, show what percentage of your time was spent on each major aspect of the job. Don't say, "Performed general secretarial duties." Be more specific. For example, you might say something like the following:

> Accepted and screened calls, responded to requests for information, received visitors (10%). Reviewed correspondence, obtained required information, replied to correspondence or routed it to proper staff member (20%). Received bulk orders of 60 different publications, organized storage, and kept inventory (25%). Prepared memoranda and letters based on notes made by supervisor (15%). Made travel arrangements for staff, prepared publications and supplies for shipment to conventions (5%). Maintained files (10%). Prepared monthly report of inquiries received, biweekly time cards, and records of time spent on duty for seven employees (10%). Kept supplies on hand (5%).

The experience blocks are not only for paid employment. Describe your volunteer work or what you have done for a family business as well.

Only one part of the description of volunteer experience differs from that of paid work: the salary block. Simply write *volunteer* there. When discussing your duties, use the same sort of language that you would if you had been paid, starting with the job's title. Be precise, neither overstating nor understating your duties.

At this point, you might be wondering how you are going to get all this information into the narrow, lined spaces provided. You can't. Type your experience, single spaced, on plain paper. Then cut out the headings (the spaces for name of employer and such) from the original, and patch the two together. The patching won't be apparent in the photocopies. This method—which has been recommended for years by the Federal Women's Program—is perfectly acceptable and results in a much cleaner looking form. It even enables you to use paragraph blocks, or special outline devices more effectively than does the original form.

All the *education and training* you have received should be listed in *Items 23–31*. Formal education will quickly come to mind, but you should also put down every workshop and seminar you have attended and every training program you have completed. Include courses taken at vocational schools and in adult education programs, training sponsored by clubs or organizations you have belonged to, and development programs paid for by your employers. In many cases, all you need to write is the title of the course, where and when you took it, and how long it lasted. But if the title of the course is vague, a very brief description of the subject matter covered is appropriate.

Items 32–36, concern *special qualifications and skills.* Mention experience in public speaking, publishing, writing, design, photography, organizing conferences, and anything else you can think of. Remembering the clubs you have belonged to and the hobbies you have engaged in may help you call to mind some of your special skills. When completing this item, you should also mention what machines you have worked with: computers, audio equipment, movie projectors, calculators, duplicators, laboratory equipment, and any other machines you have ever used. To help you remember this equipment, go back over the descriptions of your work experience and ask yourself, "What machines did I operate on that job?" In so far as possible, give the exact brand name or model of each machine. Such information will make it easier for people reading your SF-171 to picture the equipment and will also make you seem well organized.

In *Item 37,* you must name *three people* other than relatives and supervisors *who know about your ability* to do the jobs for which you are applying. Teachers, co-workers, and fellow volunteers can all give recommendations based on their knowledge of your ability. Ministers, doctors, and local politicians, though frequently used for references, are often poor choices, because they know little about how well you work. Friends are suitable references if they are in a position to evaluate your ability. About the only people you really shouldn't list are those who cannot be easily reached by a potential employer or those whom you believe might say something negative or inappropriate.

Items 38-46 are self-explanatory and regard *citizenship, convictions, termination, and retirement benefits. Item 47* is set aside as extra space. You can use it whenever you have more to say about an item than the form leaves room for. You can also continue your answers on any plain sheet of paper that is about the same size as the SF-171 or use Standard Form 171-A, which is a continuation sheet. But a cleaner SF-171 will result, as already mentioned, if you use only the headings from the SF-171 and then use blank paper for the descriptions.

Transcripts of grades can also be attached to your SF-171.

The last blank on the form is for your signature and the date. Once again, don't sign and date your master copies. Sign and date each photocopy when you send it off.

CHAPTER 4

THE JOB HUNT

The federal government is composed of various departments and agencies that vary greatly in size and purpose. The Defense Department, for example, employs over one million civilian workers. Departments such as Justice, Agriculture, and Veterans Affairs, are also large, employing over 100,000 workers each. There are also relatively small agencies, such as Education, the government Printing Office, and the Office of Personnel Management, that have fewer than 10,000 workers.

Two types of roads lead to federal jobs: *"the open highway"* and *"the hidden byways."*

THE OPEN HIGHWAY

The great advantage of the open highway to government jobs is that it's easy to find. It runs right through *the personnel office of every government agency*. The open highway begins at the *Office of Personnel Management's Federal Job Information Centers*. You will need to range far beyond the centers, however, because the Office of Personnel Management simply doesn't know everything about all the hiring going on at any one time. For example, some agencies are not even under the jurisdiction of the Office of Personnel Management; they are called *Excepted Agencies*. Some positions are also excepted from the normal procedures.

EXCEPTED AGENCIES

The *Excepted Agencies* are not free to hire and fire indiscriminately. They do establish their own procedures, however, in conformity with the laws of the United States. The largest of the excepted agencies are the *Central Intelligence Agency,* the Department of Justice's *Federal Bureau of Investigation,* the *Department of State's Foreign Service, the Nuclear Regulatory Commission,* the *General Accounting Office,* and the *Postal Service.* Employment information for most of these agencies is given in chapter 7, "The Executive Agencies," under the agency's name.

EXCEPTED POSITIONS

Excepted positions are jobs in occupations for which the Office of Personnel Management does not set the standards. The following are the excepted positions:

Doctors, dentists, and nurses employed by the Department of Medicine and Surgery, Veterans Administration.

Scientists and engineers who are employed by the National Science Foundation.

Attorneys employed by all agencies.

Chaplains, most of whom are employed by the Department of Veterans Affairs and the Department of Justice.

Teachers in Defense Department overseas schools.

Drug enforcement agents doing undercover work. (Don't apply for these positions; they are filled through recruitment.)

Part-time positions in isolated places.

Professional and Administrative Careers (PAC)

Information on most of these jobs appears in Chapter 5, "Professional, Administrative, and Scientific Careers."

Government agencies in an area are always listed in the U.S. Government section of local phone books. You can reach the personnel office simply by calling the agencies. You don't even have to leave your own home to find out about openings—or some openings, at any rate.

FINDING ANNOUNCEMENTS

Announcements concerning positions—excepted or not—are posted at the agency offering the job and through FJICs. The addresses and phone numbers for many agencies are given throughout this book. You can mail an SF-171 form to these agencies and hope to hit pay dirt. In addition, every department, and almost every agency of any size, has *regional offices* in each of the ten following cities: Boston, New York, Philadelphia, Atlanta, Chicago, Kansas City, Dallas, Denver, San Francisco, and Seattle. the regional offices are almost always faster at answering their mail than is the national office. So if you want more information about an agency, it's usually best to look in the phone book for a regional office in one of the above ten cities. The agencies are listed under *United States Government*. Then you can write to the regional office and inquire about opportunities in both the nation and your region, information the national headquarters doesn't always have.

THE JOB SERVICE

A good source of information other than the library is the *Job Service*. It is your state's employment agency, so the address of the closest office can be found under your state's name in the phone book. A well-run Job Service office will have Office of Personnel Management publications and other information about jobs with the federal government. It will also have information about jobs with state and local governments and private employers. Even if you don't know exactly what you want to do, the Job Service can help you. It has counselors who can administer aptitude tests and assist you in other ways in choosing a career.

COMMERCIAL EMPLOYMENT AGENCIES

Another way to get on the open highway through the personnel offices is by going to a *commercial employment agency*. Commercial employment agencies occasionally have information about government jobs, usually at the middle-management level. Using such agencies can be very expensive, however, so don't sign anything unless you now exactly what the agency can do for you, and you are certain that you cannot do the same thing for yourself. Some personnel agencies do not charge the job-searcher, but you should clarify the question of fees right at the start, before you get into any arrangement with them.

PUBLICATIONS

Finally, newspapers sometimes carry help-wanted ads for government agencies. For example, *The Federal Times,* a weekly newspaper, lists many announcements. It is available at 6883 Commercial Dr. , Springfield, VA 22159; (703) 750-2000. It costs $39 per year. Another publication, *Federal Career Opportunities,* contains up to 4,000 vacancy announcements per issue. It is published by the Federal Research Service, 370 Maple Avenue West, Vienna, VA 22180; (703) 281-0200. The cost for 6 issues covering a 3-month period is $37. *Federal Jobs Digest* offers a biweekly listing of the over 20,000 federal jobs available nationwide and overseas. These openings are listed by hiring agency and geographic location. Each issue also has short articles noting trends in government hiring. The *Digest* is available from Breakthrough Publications, P.O. Box 594, Millwood, NY 10546; (800) 824-5000. It costs $29 for a three month subscription, but as with the other publications mentions, the public library should receive it.

All these ways to reach the personnel offices are fairly effective in terms of finding places to send an application. You can easily contact more than 100 offices in just a few days. The major drawback to looking for jobs along the personnel office route is that personnel officers rarely know about the actual job openings available at the time you contact them. The looking is easy, but the finding is tough.

So, if you really want to find work, you may have to leave the main road and make your way along the byways.

THE HIDDEN BYWAYS

The hidden byways to government employment detour around the personnel office and lead directly to supervisors who have the authority to hire you. They are the first to learn of openings for the simple reason that the openings occur when their offices lose workers or when their offices are given the authority to hire more people. The supervisors are referred to as *hiring officials* by the Office of Personnel Management, but that is not their regular job. They are the people in middle-management who will actually supervise your work after you get on the payroll. They make their living as lawyers, engineers, or computer specialists. Hiring people is a rare task for them and it is far from simple.

STARTING YOUR SEARCH

To start your search, ask all your friends and relatives if they know anyone who does the kind of work that interests you. You may already have spoken to some potential contacts when you were deciding on an occupation. These people can often refer you to colleagues who work for the government. Or, if you already know people who work for the government, they can probably refer you to government workers in your chosen occupation.

Once you learn the names of one or more persons who hold the kind of job you want with the government, you can try to obtain an information interview. Many professionals in the career guidance field, such as authors John Crystal and Richard Bolles, advocate that job seekers try to set up this kind of an interview. People rarely mind talking about their jobs and are usually more than happy to help someone else get started. Be courteous and considerate of their time and they are not likely to feel put upon. The people you talk with will be under less pressure, because they will not have to reach a decision on whether or not to hire you when the interview ends. You want to tell the people of your interest in their field of work and ask to talk with them about it. At the interview, ask about how people get started in that occupation. Also, inquire about the names of other people you might speak with regarding a suitable position. This last question is most important.

Remember, you have to find your own way along the hidden byways. Keep asking people to point you in the right direction and be persistent. Other books on job hunting can give you more advice about these interviews.

Common courtesy is very important at this stage; a week or so after you speak to people, send them a letter thanking them for their help, enclosing a copy of your SF-171. They will be impressed; for although this advice is always given to job seekers, it is rarely taken.

If your first contact with a person is by mail instead of phone, you can send your SF-171 right away. The advantage of a letter is that you can sell yourself without actually asking for a job. Your strategy in the letter is to show your qualifications and ask the person to refer you to potential employers. The disadvantage of letters is that they are unlikely to lead to referrals or even interviews. Telephone calls are much more likely to lead to interviews and interviews are most likely to lead to referrals.

MORE WAYS TO MAKE CONTACTS

There is a chance (though it's slighter than you might imagine) that none of your friends, relatives, or relatives' friends will know anyone who does the kind of work that interests you or works for the government. In that case—and to increase your contacts even if this is not the case—you can fall back on several books.

The U.S. Government Manual, the official handbook of the U.S. government, lists the names of officials, sources of information, and the employment offices for all the government agencies. Because government job titles are often confusing, you may not be able to determine who in an agency knows about the job you want. On the other hand, you often can. For example, if you're interested in a supply job and you see "Deputy Assistant Secretary for Grant and Procurement Management," you will know whom to start with. That person will probably be too high up to do the actual hiring for entry-level position, but he or she might be able to refer you to those who do. After your conversation, send a thank-you note and an SF-171; the Deputy Assistant Secretary might circulate it around the agency. Should no name in the *Manual* look promising, you will have to make a few stabs in the dark. Call the agency's information or personnel office and ask whoever answers for the name of someone engaged in your kind of work. (The lists of major employers for each occupation in the jobs chapter and the descriptions of the agencies in the agency chapter should point you toward which agencies to contact first.) Eventually, you will find someone who can help you, though it may take many phone calls. By the way, this approach generally works best with the small agencies.

CHAPTER 5

PROFESSIONAL, ADMINISTRATIVE, AND SCIENTIFIC CAREERS

The range of services the federal government must provide is as wide as its responsibilities. No single book can describe all the jobs that three million people do. But the jobs of most federal workers are described in this chapter, the next one, and the one on the Postal Service.

Each entry in this chapter and the next gives the job's title, the numerical code by which the occupation is listed in government manuals and collections of vacancy announcements, the job's major duties, and the education or skills required for entry. The number of people employed, where they are concentrated geographically, and the agencies that employ the most workers in the occupation are also sometimes stated in order to give you some idea of your chances for employment in the field. Because job titles can be misleading, it is a good idea to glance over occupations you have not previously considered. They might offer good opportunities, and you might be qualified for them.

This chapter concerns professional, administrative, and scientific careers—the ones usually entered by college graduates, although people with the right kind of experience also qualify for them. The jobs are discussed in alphabetical order. Each position included here offers opportunities for at least 5,000 persons. A list of some occupations with fewer than 5,000 employees appears at the end of the chapter. But before turning to the particular occupations, it might be worthwhile to make a few general comments about the classification system, pay grades, and job requirements.

THE PERSONNEL CLASSIFICATION SYSTEM

The Government's Personnel Classification System includes an Occupational Group structure that places like jobs together. There are 22 Occupational Groups, ranging from GS-100 to GS-2100. Below is a list of Federal Occupation Groups.

Occupational Group Number	*Occupational Group Title*
GS-000	Miscellaneous
GS-100	Social Science, Psychology and Welfare
GS-200	Personnel Management and Industrial Relations
GS-300	Administrative, Clerical and Office Services
GS-400	Biological Sciences
GS-500	Accounting and Budget
GS-600	Medical, Hospital, Dental and Public Health
GS-700	Veterinary Medical Science
GS-800	Engineering and Architecture
GS-900	Legal and Kindred
GS-1000	Information and Arts
GS-1100	Business and Industry
GS-1200	Copyright, Patent and Trademark
GS-1300	Physical Sciences
GS-1400	Library and Archives
GS-1500	Mathematics and Statistics
GS-1600	Equipment, Facilities and Service
GS-1700	Education
GS-1800	Investigation
GS-1900	Quality Assurance, Inspection and Grading
GS-2000	Supply
GS-2100	Transportation

Each Occupational Group has a three-part identifier; the Pay System, Occupational Group Number, and Title. In the example, GS-400, Biological Sciences, GS means the job is in the General Schedule (white collar) pay system; 400 is the group number; and Biological Sciences is the group title.

Federal government employees almost always fall into a certain pay grade. All the jobs in this chapter are in what is called the *General Schedule* (GS). Grades in the General Schedule go from GS-1 to GS-18. Almost all the occupations described here start at GS-5, which denotes a salary similar to those offered to new college graduates by private companies. The lower grades are assigned to clerical and technical employees, whose jobs are described in the next chapter. More information about grades and pay is given in Chapter 11, "Salary and Other Benefits."

Now, let's look at the jobs themselves.

SPECIFIC POSITIONS

Accountants and auditors (GS510) keep track of how much money an agency spends and receives. They also evaluate the performance of contractors and offices within the agency to make sure that the taxpayers get what they pay for. They are found in almost every agency. Some agencies are responsible for auditing the work of many other agencies and, therefore, employ large numbers of accountants and auditors. These auditing agencies include the Air Force Audit Agency, the Army Audit Agency, the Defense Contract Audit Agency, the Navy Audit Agency, and the General Accounting Office. The Departments of Agriculture, Treasury, Health and Human Services, and Energy also employ large numbers of the government's accountants and auditors, about one-fourth of whom work in Washington. To qualify for these positions, applicants should have majored in accounting or taken at least 24 semester hours of college-level courses in accounting or auditing. Many government accountants are Certified Public Accountants.

Administrative assistants and officers (GS341) have many different duties, depending on their particular job. They might almost be thought of as the people who manage an office so that others can do the work required of the agency by Congress and the President. For example, the function of NASA is the exploration of outer space and many of its employees work directly on that task; but, in order for them to do their work, administrative assistants in the agency organize the inner space of the office building, manage the hiring and paying of employees, administer contracts, arrange for office supplies and computer equipment, provide for office security, and take care of any number of other necessary—albeit glamourless—tasks.

Because the duties of administrative officers are so varied, these employees usually specialize in a particular aspect of a job. Entry positions (GS-5) are open to college graduates regardless of major. Administrative officers are employed throughout the government. Only the Defense Department and Postal Service employ more than 1,000, but each of the large agencies employs a substantial number.

Aerospace engineers: See Engineers in this chapter.

Air traffic control specialists (GS2152) make sure that planes don't fly into each other. They are the "tower" that the pilot talks to when taking off or landing, and the control centers that tell pilots where to fly when going from one point to another. They must keep track of several planes at once, and they must be able to keep calm and make decisions quickly in an emergency. Consider the number of planes that hover around a major airport like so many bees converging on a hive, and you will realize just how stressful an occupation air traffic control is. The work is so demanding, in fact, that applicants must meet stricter physical requirements than usual for federal jobs.

Applicants for terminal and center specialties must not have reached their 31st birthday. All applicants must have 20/20 vision, at least with the use of glasses; they must also have excellent peripheral vision. Applicants must have excellent hearing and the ability to speak clearly and concisely. They must have a medical history free of heart disease, diabetes mellitus, and mental disorders. All must pass written and oral examinations. A college degree is required of most applicants, but experience can be substituted for education if the experience is related to air traffic control. Acceptable experience includes things such as providing pilots with information about weather and airport conditions or doing research on new air traffic control systems. Despite the strict requirements for this occupation, competition for these jobs is intense.

Air traffic control specialists work at airports and control centers throughout the United States. Since planes are in the air around the clock, shift-work is required. Most of the controllers are employed by the Federal Aviation Administration, which is part of the Department of Transportation; but the Army, Navy, and Air Force also employ at least two hundred civilians each in this job. To make sure that all airports and control centers are adequately staffed, air traffic controllers may have to move from one city to another.

Attorneys: See Lawyers in this chapter.

Budget analysts or officers (GS560) see that an agency spends no more than Congress said it could. Putting together a budget for an agency is a complicated business. Every agency has many different programs, and the people in charge of each one estimate how much money their program needs. Budget analysts review these estimates and plan one budget for the whole agency. They also review requests for funds throughout the year, ensuring that the requests don't exceed the amount of money available. Finally, they regularly evaluate the cost of a program in relation to its success.

A college degree qualifies people for GS-5. Budget clerks and accounting technicians may be promoted into these positions. Budget analysts work for just about every agency, the larger agencies naturally employing more of them. More than one-third of the government's estimated 9,800 budget analysts and officers work in Washington.

Chemists (GS1320) study the nature of the elements and their components—the way they are put together, their properties, and the way they interact with each other. The Office of Personnel Management used to say, "Highly advanced government programs of research and investigation are of such diversity of approach and interest as to include practically any special preferences a prospective employee may have." In other words, no matter what problems chemists wish to solve, the federal government probably has jobs for them.

Chemists qualify for entry positions (GS-5) on the basis of their education. A college degree is required for most positions, including 30 semester hours in chemistry and 6 in physics. Chemists, the largest group of scientists in the government, work for a variety of agencies.

Civil engineers: See Engineers in this chapter.

Civil rights analysts (GS160) conduct research on voting rights, housing, and other civil rights issues and recommend policies for the government to implement. A bachelor's degree in any field qualifies an applicant for the entry level (GS-5). These workers are widely dispersed among the various governmental agencies.

Computer specialists (GS334) include computer programmers, computer systems analysts, and computer equipment analysts. These three occupations are closely related, and the performance of any one of them requires substantial knowledge of the others.

Programmers write detailed instructions for the computer so that it can accomplish a given task one step at a time. The instructions, or programs, are harder to write than one might imagine, because the computers, though very fast, are very dumb. Every instruction must be presented to the computer in an either/or format; it cannot choose among three or more possibilities.

Systems analysts are usually responsible for determining which agency tasks can be accomplished by the computer. They do not actually write programs, but they must know whether or not a particular job can be programmed.

Equipment analysts study the kinds of work an agency does and determine what kind of computer equipment the agency should purchase.

College graduates are usually hired for entry-level positions in these occupations. Courses in data processing are helpful, but not required. Many positions require people with special knowledge of the subject that the computers will deal with, such as physics or mathematics.

The federal government pioneered the development of computers and is still the largest single user of computer systems. The Departments of Treasury, Defense, and Health and Human Services employ large numbers of computer specialists; however, computer specialists can be found in nearly every agency.

Contact representative (GS962) is one of those job titles that keeps the job's duties a secret. These workers might better be called ''explainers,'' because they explain government programs to people. For example, contact representatives who work for the Treasury Department tell people how to figure their taxes and contact representatives who work for the Department of Health and Human Services explain social security benefits to people.

College graduates are usually recruited for these positions (even though the Office of Personnel Management classifies them as technical), but you can qualify for the lower grades (GS-4) with only two years of education after high school. These jobs are widely scattered throughout the United States; there are only about 200 contact representatives in Washington.

Contract and procurement specialists (GS1102) buy goods and services that other government workers need in order to do their jobs. This is, perhaps, one occupation that people considering a government career rarely think of; and yet, some 21,000 people are employed as contract and procurement specialists. When the government needs to purchase something—and it purchases billions of dollars worth of goods and services each year—someone has to make sure that the taxpayers get the best buy for their money. This responsibility rests with contract and procurement specialists. Some contracts—one with a printer for a single publication, for example—are fairly simple. Other projects—building a new jet fighter plane, for instance—require complex negotiations and careful administration.

College graduates are preferred no matter what their majors. Contract and procurement specialists work in every agency, but the Armed Forces, Defense Logistics Agency, and General Services Administration are among the larger employers.

Criminal investigators (GS1810 and GS1811) ask "Who done it?" When a law has been broken, the investigators gather evidence, talk to witnesses, trail suspects, and make arrests. The work is physically difficult, involves personal risks, demands considerable travel, and requires irregular, unscheduled hours. It is a demanding occupation that offers a variety of challenges as well as good opportunities for advancement.

Applicants must be at least 21 years old. A college degree, in any field, is usually required, but law school graduates are preferred. Almost every large agency employs a few criminal investigators, but about half work for the Department of Justice, and several thousand work for the Department of the Treasury, which includes the Bureau of Alcohol, Tobacco, and Firearms, the U.S. Customs Service, and the Internal Revenue Service (IRS).

Economists (GS110) keep track of the way people spend their money, which means that they study what people buy and how much they pay for products. They also estimate how large a supply there is of things to buy. Economists with the government use this information for two purposes: to regulate prices and to determine policies that will help the country's economy grow. For example, if a company that sells electric power across state lines wants to raise its rates, economists in the

Federal Power Commission must determine if the rate increase is fair. Or, if unemployment or inflation rates are high, economists try to figure out how to bring them down. Of course, such policy decisions are made only at the highest level of government and must be approved by Congress and the President. Economists at lower levels might be principally engaged in finding out what the unemployment rates actually are, among other things.

The lowest grade for economists is GS-5. College graduates with 21 semester hours in economics and 3 in statistics, accounting, or calculus qualify. Economists work for a large number of agencies, but the Department of Labor and Agriculture have the most.

Electrical/electronics engineers: See Engineers in this chapter.

Engineers (GS800 series)—more than 90,000 strong—are among the most numerous employees in the federal service. By and large, engineers are employed by almost every agency, and the jobs are scattered throughout the country. In general, people qualify for GS-5 entry-level positions if (a) they have graduated from a school of engineering; (b) they are registered as professional engineers; (c) they have completed 60 semester hours in an engineering curriculum and have had one year of professional experience; or (d) they have passed the written test required for professional registration or have passed the *Engineer-in-Training Examination*. (The Engineer-in-Training Examination is administered by the Board of Engineering Examiners in each state. *Do not write the Office of Personnel Management or any other federal agency for information; write to the Secretary of your state's Board.*)

Since there are so many different types of engineering, it might be helpful to examine the duties of the major engineering fields separately. Among the specialized engineers employed by the federal government are *aerospace engineers, civil engineers, electronics* and *electrical engineers,* and *mechanical engineers.*

Aerospace engineers gave us wings and took us to the moon. Planes, helicopters, and rockets fly above us because of their work, which includes designing and developing aircraft and spacecraft for optimal performance. Most of these employees, naturally, are with the National Aeronautics and Space Administration, Air Force, and Navy.

Civil engineers plan military bases, roads, and dams. The Army Corps of Engineers employs more than 9,000 engineers—6,000 of them civil engineers—which makes the Corps "the largest concentration of professional construction talent in the world," according to the Office of Personnel Management. Other major employers include the Department of Transportation and its Federal Highway Administration, the Department of Agriculture, the Navy, and the Department of the Interior, which is responsible for many of the dams and canals built in this country.

Electronics and electrical engineers design the equipment that keeps the American government in touch with the world, whether it be an ordinary telephone line or a sophisticated radar device. Although electronics and electrical engineers might work on the design and manufacture of any kind of electrical equipment, most of those employed in the federal service are concerned with communications equipment. The major employers are the Armed Forces, the National Aeronautics and Space Administration, and the Coast Guard, which is part of the Department of Transportation.

Mechanical engineers work with engines, some that power a ship through ice floes in the North Atlantic and some that merely air condition an office building in New Mexico. The Armed Forces are the largest employers, but almost every agency employs at least a few mechanical engineers.

Equipment specialists (GS1670) are administrators and technicians who approve designs, negotiate contracts, and instruct people in the use of equipment. They must be able to read blueprints and understand technical language, and they must have a practical knowledge of equipment and mechanics. They are usually specialists in a particular kind of equipment, such as aircraft, missiles, or ships. Positions start at GS-5, for which a college degree in engineering, physics, or a related subject is qualifying. The Defense Department employs almost all of the equipment specialists in the government.

FBI special agents really do shoot guns and take part in surprise raids on criminal headquarters, but much of their work is far less exciting. They are investigators, and their job requires that they look for evidence when a crime is suspected. They interview witnesses, examine records, and keep watch over suspects. They are on call 24 hours a day, may have to travel anywhere in the United States, and frequently work overtime. These jobs are hard to obtain because the turnover of agents is low and the requirements are high. Lawyers and accountants are the preferred applicants, although physicists, language specialists, and experienced police officers are sometimes hired. Applicants must be between the ages of 23 and 35 and pass a rigid physical examination. The only employer of agents is the Federal Bureau of Investigation, which has almost 60 field offices located throughout the country. Agents are attached to a particular field office, so the jobs are widely scattered.

Financial institution examiners (GS570) audit savings and loan associations, credit unions, farm credit associations, cooperative banks, investment firms, national banks, and other financial institutions. To perform an audit, examiners study the assets or holdings of the institution and determine their value. Then the examiners balance the assets against the institution's liabilities, that is, the money it owes to people and other institutions.

Applicants with a college degree can qualify for most entry-level positions (GS-5) if they have 24 semester hours in business-related subjects. Between them, the Federal Deposit Insurance Corporation and the Department of the Treasury employ almost all of the government's examiners, but a few work for such small, specialized agencies as the Farm Credit Administration. Very few of these jobs are located in Washington; most require extensive travel from city to city within a region.

Foresters (GS460) take care of forests, a simple statement that doesn't do justice to the complicated task of managing more than 100 million acres of federal property. (That is an area larger than any of the states except Texas and Alaska.) America's forests serve many ends. They must be available for recreation, and they must also yield wood and other products for fuel, building material, and the paper on which this and other books are printed. Foresters are responsible for seeing that the woodlands are as productive as possible while protected from fire, disease, and erosion.

College graduates qualify as foresters (GS-5) if they have majored in subjects such as forestry, silviculture (the development and care of forests), and range management. No exam is necessary. Competition is usually keen for these positions, most of which are with the *Department of Agriculture's Forest Service*. The Department of the Interior and several other agencies also employ foresters.

Internal revenue officers (GS1169) see that people pay their taxes. They review the tax returns of private citizens and corporations whose claims are unusual for some reason—for example, because they gave an uncommonly large sum of money to charity. The agents next look over the taxpayer's financial records and, if necessary, try to collect information from other sources. Agents also advise taxpayers and government attorneys about tax matters and prepare rulings concerning taxes.

To qualify, a college graduate must have taken at least 24 semester hours in accounting and auditing. All the government's internal revenue agents work for the *Treasury Department*. According to the Office of Personnel Management, "A very substantial portion of the top executive positions in the various Internal Revenue Service offices throughout the country are held by persons who began their careers as agents." Only a few hundred agents work in Washington; the rest are assigned to the 60 district offices located around the country.

Inventory managers: See Supply Management Specialists in this chapter.

Lawyers (GS905) are critical to the effectiveness of the government, which, after all, tries to ensure the safety and welfare of Americans by enacting and enforcing laws that require or forbid certain acts. Lawyers become involved both when the laws are written and when they are broken.

Lawyers are among the workers who are not hired through the Office of Personnel Managment. When an agency needs lawyers, it looks for them itself. Applicants must have an LL.B. or J.D. degree and pass their state's bar exam before they are hired. Degree holders who have not passed the bar exam may be hired as law clerks; law clerks must then pass the bar within 14 months of being hired or they will be fired.

Every government agency hires lawyers, but the Departments of Justice and the Treasury together employ about one-third of the government's general attorneys. The regulatory agencies, such as the Securities and Exchange Commission and the Equal Employment Opportunities Commission, also employ many lawyers. Although government lawyers work throughout the country, almost half of them are stationed in or near Washington.

Loan specialists (GS1165) examine and analyze financial factors and credit risks, counsel loan applicants, and investigate problems with repayment.

The qualification standards do not specify any particular college courses as being required for the GS-5 level, but the phrase "ability to gather and analyze facts and figures" might be interpreted to mean that an applicant should have taken some finance or accounting courses. The government's loan specialists are concentrated in three agencies: Agriculture, Housing and Urban Development, and the Small Business Administration. Few of the positions are located in Washington.

Management analysts (GS343) study the way an office is organized. They interview the employees, learn what work has to be done, and discover what procedures are followed. They then make a report recommending improvements in the organization of the office. College graduates are usually hired for beginning jobs in this field. Analyst positions are found in all the larger agencies.

Mechanical engineers: See Engineers in this chapter.

Medical officers: See Physicians in this chapter.

Nurses (GS610) care for the sick and injured. Except for doctors, they are the most highly trained health professionals and have the widest range of jobs. About 35,000 nurses work for the federal government, making them the largest group of professional employees in the federal service after engineers.

The kind of patients treated and, therefore, the kind of work nurses do, depends largely on whether they are employed by a large hospital or small clinic. A large hospital—such as the 150 or so run by the Department of Veterans Affairs, and the many others run by the Armed Forces and the Public Health Service—offers a great variety of jobs for clinical nurses. At such a hospital, one nurse may work in an intensive care unit, while another works in orthopedics or surgery. Health clinics located in government office buildings employ occupational nurses who treat people who become sick or are injured on the job. Occupational nurses also practice preventive medicine, which means they test people for illness before any symptoms exist and suggest diets and activities for continued health.

To qualify for a government job, an applicant must be a *registered nurse*. Since health and illness are not limited to any one geographic area, there are government jobs for nurses all over the country. To learn about local opportunities, first find out what federal hospitals are located near where you live. Their names will be listed in the telephone book under *U.S. Government.* Then write or call the personnel office of the hospital.

Personnel management specialists (GS201) hire, promote, and train the government's labor force. Despite their title, these employees are less specialized than other kinds of personnel administrators; their jobs combine the duties of two or more of the following personnel workers: personnel staffing specialists, position classification specialists, employee development specialists, labor-management relations specialists, and employee relations specialists. An individual personnel management specialist might interview people looking for a job, review a supervisor's recommendation that someone be promoted, determine the pay scale for a particular job, plan training programs, or try to settle disputes between supervisors and those who work under them.

College graduates qualify for entry-level positions. Only the Army employs over 1,000 personnel management specialists, but almost every agency employs some.

Physicians, called medical officers (GS602) by government agencies, treat patients, conduct research, and advise government officials on health-related subjects. To qualify, applicants must usually be graduates of medical schools who have finished their internships and are licensed to practice, although some residencies and internships are available.

The vast majority of the physicians employed by the federal government work for the *Department of Veterans Affairs* in the *Department of Medicine and Surgery,* although the *Department of Health and Human Services* also employs several thousand, mostly in the *Public Health Service* and the *National Institute of Health.*

Physicists (GS1310) study the laws of nature that control matter, motion, and energy. Some specialize in the use or control of atomic energy, others in atmospheric phenomena, others in electricity, and still others in a variety of more specialized fields. All applicants must have taken at least 24 semester hours of college-level courses in subjects such as electricity and magnetism, heat, light, mechanics, sound, and other aspects of physics. Many positions are open only to applicants who have graduate degrees.

About a score of agencies employ the government's physicists, including such unexpected ones as the Department of Commerce, to which the National Bureau of Standards and the National Weather Service belong. The Navy and the Army employ the most physicists.

Production controllers (GS1152) are concerned with the manufacture and repair of equipment. When the equipment can be made or repaired by use of mechanical production methods, production controllers are in charge of planning the process and estimating its cost. College graduates qualify for a GS-5 rating in this occupation. Most of the production controllers work for the Navy, Air Force, and Army.

Program analysts (GS345) determine how well the government works by evaluating particular programs and recommending improvements. "Program," a rather vague word, can refer to a project as vast and complex as building the Space Shuttle or as relatively simple as collecting information about the amount of wheat being grown this year. In order to do their work, program analysts must determine the purpose of the program, its cost, and its success in fulfilling its purpose.

Program analysts need experience in management analysis, statistics and financial management. They are fairly high-level employees. Positions start at GS-9, which, in general, means that a college graduate must have had at least two years of experience in order to qualify. The government has over 13,500 program analysts spread throughout dozens of agencies.

Programmers: See Computer Specialists in this chapter.

Quality assurance specialists (GS1910) make sure that everything bought by the government is as good as it should be. To do this, they are stationed in the manufacturer's plant, so that problems can be spotted before the finished product is delivered. To qualify, an applicant must be a college graduate who majored in fields such as business, engineering, and production management. The Army, Navy, Air Force, and Defense Logistics Agency employ almost all of these workers.

Social insurance representatives and administrators (GS105) explain the social security program to the general public, interview claimants, and review claims. College graduates qualify for the entry-level (GS-5), no matter what their major. All work for the *Department of Health and Human Services,* and all but about two hundred work outside Washington.

Social insurance claims examiners (GS993) assist people filing for social security benefits. They interview people making claims, obtain the information needed, and explain the social insurance program to the general public. A college education qualifies people for GS-5.

These jobs are numerous (over 11,000), located throughout the United States (more than 1,300 local offices), and are easy to learn about, because all but a few are offered by a single agency, the *Social Security Administration of the Department of Health and Human Services.*

Supply management specialists (GS2003) and *inventory management specialists* (GS2010) are in charge of seeing that government employees have the material they need to do their jobs at the lowest cost to the taxpayers. Specialists must figure out how much of everything is needed; buy it, store it, and distribute it. Any college graduate can qualify. The *Defense Department,* which includes the Defense Logistics Agency, is the largest employer of these workers.

Systems analysts: See Computer Specialists in this chapter.

Teachers (GS1710) One of the largest American school systems is not even in the United States. It is in the score of foreign countries where American servicemen and women are stationed with their families. The schools in this system, administered by the *Department of Defense Dependents' Schools,* offer classes from kindergarten through the senior year of high school. They employ the same types of teachers, counselors, librarians, and administrators found in schools located in this country. Another large school system run by the United States government is under the direction of the *Department of the Interior's Bureau of Indian Affairs.* These schools are located on Indian reservations. Many of the teachers in these schools work more than 30 miles from the nearest large town.

Teachers qualify for jobs in the schools run by the government on the basis of their education and experience. In general, they must have a college degree and at least 18 semester hours of education courses, plus additional course work in elementary education or their subject specialty.

Training instructors (GS1712) make a living teaching other people how to make a living. They are the instructors in occupational, trade, and craftworker training programs run by the federal government. In general, training instructors must have practical and teaching experience in the trade they are going to teach even for the lowest pay grade (GS-5). The Army and the Air Force employ the largest number of these workers, very few of whom work in the nation's capital.

OTHER OCCUPATIONS

A complete list of the professional, administrative, and scientific jobs in the federal government would be about as long as a list of these jobs in the private sector. Such a list would not serve any purpose here, however, because very few people are employed in many of those occupations and, in most cases, there is intense competition for the few openings that exist. The following list, therefore, is restricted to occupations in which 1,000 or more people are employed.

Agricultural management specialist GS475
Appraiser GS1171
Architect GS808
Aviation safety officer GS1825
Biologist GS5401
Cartographer GS1370
Communications manager and management specialist GS391
Consumer safety officer GS696
Correctional officer GS007
Customs inspector GS1890
Dental officer GS680
Dietitian GS630
Digital computer systems administrator GS330
Educational assistant, education officer, educational specialist, and
    advisor in education GS1720
Employee development specialist GS235
Employee relations specialist GS230
Environmental protection specialist GS028
Facility manager GS1640
Financial analysis assistant GS1160
Financial manager GS505
Fingerprint clerk and fingerprint examiner GS072

Fishery biologist GS482
Food assistance program specialist GS120
Foreign affairs analyst GS130
Foreign service information officer GS1085
General health science workers GS601
General inspection, investigation, and compliance workers GS1801
Geologist GS1350
Housing manager GS1173
Hydrologist GS1315
Immigration inspector and examiner GS1816
Import specialist GS1889
Industrial specialist GS1150
Intelligence research specialist and operation specialist GS132
Labor relations specialist GS233
Librarian GS1410
Logistics management specialist GS346
Manpower development specialist GS142
Mathematician GS1520
Medical technologist GS644
Meteorologist GS406
Microbiologist GS403
Military personnel specialist GS205
Park ranger and park manager GS025
Personnel staffing specialist GS212
Pharmacist GS660
Physical scientist GS1301
Plant protection and quarantine officer GS436
Position classification specialist GS221
Printing management officer GS1654
Program manager (title varies with program) GS340
Property utilization, marketing, or disposal specialist GS1104
Psychologist GS180
Public health program specialist GS685
Public information officer GS1081
Range conservationist and range scientist GS454
Realty officer GS1170
Recreation/therapeutic recreation specialist GS188

Safety management specialist GS018
Security administration officer GS080
Social science analyst GS101
Social worker GS185
Soil conservationist GS457
Soil scientist GS470
Statistician GS1530
Supply cataloger GS2050
Support services administrator GS342
Technical writer/editor GS1083
Traffic manager and traffic management officer GS2130
Transportation specialist GS2101
Veterans claims examiner GS99
Veterinary medical officer GS701
Visual information officer GS1084
Wage and hour compliance specialist GS249
Wildlife biologist GS486
Writer/editor GS1082

CHAPTER 6

CLERICAL, TECHNICAL, AND BLUE-COLLAR CAREERS

Clerical, technical, and blue-collar workers assist government administrators, scientists, and other professional-level employees. This chapter describes occupations in these fields that employ at least 10,000 workers and lists many others. As with the previous chapter, each entry gives the job's title, the numerical code by which it is listed in government manuals and collections of vacancy announcements, the general duties and qualifications, the number employed, and the major employers.

Here is some general information about the kinds of work done in these fields.

CLERICAL OCCUPATIONS

Clerical occupations usually involve office work: typing, keeping records, and processing forms. Clerical workers make up by far the largest group of government employees. There are almost 400,000 in the executive agencies, and they are always in short supply. These jobs are in the *General Schedule* (GS). Most start at GS-2, which usually requires a high school diploma, but some begin at GS-1.

Clerical occupations offer people good opportunities for advancement for two reasons. First, the government has many training programs of which clerical workers can take advantage. Second, hiring new people is a complicated process in the government; firing old ones is even harder. When possible, supervisors much prefer promoting a well-qualified person whose habits and abilities are known to hiring from the outside. This way, the supervisor runs less risk of being stuck with a marginal worker who isn't very efficient, but cannot be fired for incompetence. Of course, not every clerk becomes an administrator, and many clerical positions are rather dull. But clerical jobs do offer talented people—including college graduates—a way to get into the system and then move up.

TECHNICAL OCCUPATIONS

Technical occupations are those frequently called *paraprofessional*. The work involves fewer routine tasks and requires practical knowledge of a specialized subject. Technical workers often start at GS-4 and can either advance in their technical specialty or move into the professional, scientific, or administrative area to which their work is related. Additional formal education may be needed to make such a move.

BLUE-COLLAR WORKERS

Blue-collar workers are defined by the type of work they do, not the difficulty of the work. Many of these workers are very highly skilled and become proficient in their craft only after years of experience. The pay scale for these workers is very different from that of other federal employees. Secretaries and scientists who work for the government make the same amount of money whether they live in Washington, D.C., or Washington State. But the wages of government blue-collar workers vary from place to place, so that the wage will be about the same as that of other blue-collar workers in the surrounding area. This pay scale is called the *Wage Board Schedule* (WG). Most government workers are under the *General Schedule* (GS). Grades in the Wage Board Schedule go from WG-1 to WG-15. WG-10 is the equivalent of journeyworker status for most blue-collar occupations. One way to become a journeyworker is through an apprenticeship program. Apprenticeships usually require four years of on-the-job training and classroom work, which shows how demanding many of these occupations are.

Blue-collar occupations are one group in which the variety of jobs offered by the government does not equal that of private industry; many blue-collar jobs are in manufacturing, and the government does not manufacture much. Nevertheless, many opportunities still exist for the blue-collar worker, as almost one half-million workers can attest. Just three agencies—the Navy, Army, and Air Force—employ about 7 out of 10 of the government's blue-collar workers. The Postal Service is also a major employer of these workers.

To qualify for a blue-collar position, applicants must be able to do the work required for the particular job; length of experience or training doesn't matter. People not qualified for the journeyworker level can be hired as trades helpers. Trades helpers perform jobs in which the following skills are learned: how to use tools properly, read blueprints and technical manuals, make adjustments, and rebuild and make parts. Helpers who are usually under the direction of a journeyworker, have a grade WG-5 rating.

SPECIFIC POSITIONS

Accounting technicians (GS525) do for the government what bookkeepers do for the rest of the country. They keep records, prepare reports, and balance the books—that is, they check how much money is owed to the agency, compared to how much the agency owes.

To qualify, applicants should have at least two years of education after high school. A test is required for the lowest entry position, GS-4, but not for the next higher grade, which requires a college degree. The experience that accounting technicians receive on the job may make it possible for them to advance into professional accounting positions.

These jobs are spread all over the United States. Nearly all the agencies employ accounting technicians, but the largest employers are the Department of Defense, Treasury, and Agriculture.

Aircraft mechanics (WS8852) do for airplanes what the local automotive mechanic does for cars: they keep them working. Aircraft mechanics find out what is wrong with the plane, remove worn or broken parts, and put everything back together. They start at grade WG-10. Aircraft workers have a lower rating and perform simpler tasks than mechanics. The Air Force employs about 10,000 aircraft mechanics; the Navy and Army employ more than 2,000 each.

Claims clerks (GS998) see that people get what is coming to them from benefit programs, such as Social Security. They examine the person's claim, checking to make sure that the right information is included and that the claim has been made in time. More than 7,000 claims clerks work for the Department of Health and Human Services, which includes the Social Security Administration, and more than 1,000 work for the Department of Veterans Affairs. The rest are scattered among several agencies. The jobs are located throughout the United States. In fact, there are only a few hundred claims clerks in Washington. The lowest grade is GS-2, for which high school graduates can qualify if they pass a test.

Clerks (GS300 series and GS500 series) number in the hundreds of thousands in the federal government; the Army alone employs nearly 30,000. Clerks check records and documents, put together information based on the records and documents, and provide information to the general public about the office in which they work. In addition to general clerks, the government employs many other clerical workers whose jobs are described elsewhere in this chapter. (See the following job titles: clerk-typists, data transcribers, mail and file clerks, reporting stenographers and shorthand reporters, and secretaries.)

Applicants must be interested in clerical work and show that they can be successful at the job. High school graduates qualify for the GS-2. A test is given for this grade and for all higher ones. As with general clerks, many of the other clerical positions require little or no experience and only a high school diploma; some, however, such as reporting stenographer, require considerable skill.

Clerks who wish to move up to professional or administrative jobs can take advantage of the government's training programs or take college courses and have their tuition paid by the government.

Clerk-stenographers: See Reporting Stenographers and Shorthand Reporters in this chapter.

Clerk-typists (GS322) are employed by the thousands by the Army, Air Force, Navy, Defense Logistics Agency, Department of Veterans

Affairs, Tennessee Valley Authority, and the Departments of Treasury, Justice, the Interior, Agriculture, Labor, Health and Human Services, Housing and Urban Development, and Transportation. Total employment exceeds 60,000.

A high school diploma qualifies applicants for the entry-level position (GS-2). Applicants should be able to type 40 words a minute. No typing test is given; however, during a probationary period, new clerk-typists must show their ability to the satisfaction of their supervisor. A general test is required, which deals with verbal and clerical aptitude.

Computer operators (GS332) load the computer with magnetic tapes or disks for a particular program or operation, start the machine, and watch while it processes the program. The operators look for signs that the computer is not working properly; if it is not, they find the source of the trouble and fix it or call the service technician.

All applicants must pass a written test. A high school diploma or a 200- or 300-hour computer-training course qualifies applicants for the lowest grade (GS-2). Training courses are offered by a large variety of schools. If you consider taking one, remember that *no school is licensed by the Office of Personnel Management,* and *no school can guarantee that you will get any job,* much less a government job, when you finish the course.

Computer operators work in almost every agency, but the large majority are with the Departments of Defense and the Treasury. Computers must also operate around the clock because people in the government need constant access to the information they analyze. As a result, computer operators must often be available for work at night and on weekends.

Data transcribers (GS356) talk to computers. Computers can't hear, of course, so the conversation takes place through punched cards, magnetic tapes, and disks. Data transcribers, working at machines that have keyboards similar to a typewriter's, transfer information and directions onto the tapes or disks that are fed into the machine by computer operators. Transcribers also do general clerical work when necessary.

No experience, education, or training is required for the lowest grade (GS-1). Employees at this grade do simple, repetitive transcribing. For GS-2, the next higher grade, applicants must pass a test and have a high school diploma. The Departments of the Treasury, Defense, and Health and Human Services employ the bulk of these workers.

Electricians (WG2805) install and repair the electric wiring in offices, hospitals, warehouses, and other buildings. They have to be able to fix electrical fixtures, distribution panels, conduit wiring, high voltage outlets, searchlights, and electrical appliances; but they don't work on outside power lines. Electricians are sometimes exposed to cuts, burns, and electric shocks. More than half the 13,000 electricians employed by the federal government work for the Navy, and both the Army and the Air Force employ more than a thousand.

Electronics mechanics (WG2604) install and repair radar, missile control, and other sophisticated equipment. They use both simple hand tools and complicated testing devices such as oscilloscopes to do their work. People qualify for these positions solely on the ability to do the work. Although electronics mechanics are a fairly large group of workers—there are about 17,000—almost all of them work for the Defense Department.

Electronics technicians (GS856) work with medical equipment, radar, radio transmitters, and computers. Some operate this machinery, while others test it or determine what is wrong with it when it doesn't work. Electronics technicians must know algebra, elementary physics, and basic electronics. To qualify, they must have at least two years of schooling after high school in subjects such as electronics, engineering, physics, and mathematics. Repairing television sets is one kind of experience that qualifies people to be electronics technicians. The Department of Transportation alone employs 8,000 of these workers; another 6,000 work for the Navy; and another 7,000 work at other agencies, notably the Army and Air Force.

Engineering aides and technicians (GS802) test equipment, operate laboratory instruments, and prepare reports. This occupation has a very wide grade spread, going all the way from GS-1 to GS-15. In the lower grades, aides are closely supervised by engineers or scientists and do simple, repetitive work. At the higher levels, they do work similar to that of professional engineers.

The general experience required of applicants gives a good idea of the nature of the work. The following are among the kinds of work that are applicable as related experience: (a) apprenticeship training that included drafting and mechanical drawing; (b) surveying experience (chain or rod) as a surveyor's helper; (c) work as a drafter; or (d) experience as a laboratory mechanic or aide. Specialized experience is also required. A high school graduate qualifies for GS-2; additional technical education qualifies applicants for higher grades. Neither experience nor education is required for GS-1, but there are fewer than a hundred such positions.

Engineering aides and technicians are employed all around the country. Almost all the larger agencies employ some; the Navy, Air Force, National Aeronautics and Space Administration, and the Departments of Agriculture, Transportation, and the Interior each employs more than 1,000.

Financial administration workers (GS503) perform or supervise accounting, budgeting, and financial management tasks that cannot be more specifically classified. The lowest grade is GS-1, but most workers are hired at higher levels. The government employs about 11,600 workers in this category, each of the following employing at least a thousand: Treasury, Army, Navy, Air Force.

File clerks: See Mail and File Clerks in this chapter.

Firefighters and other fire protection workers (GS081) combat fires on ships and airfields and in buildings and industrial plants. In addition to firefighters, this group of workers includes fire communications operators (who work telephone, telegraph, and radio equipment), fire protection inspectors (who locate and remove fire hazards), fire protection specialists (who plan fire prevention programs), and fire chiefs (who supervise the firefighters and other workers).

Applicants must pass a written test and a test of stamina and agility for the entry-level grade (GS-3). Many physical conditions may disqualify an applicant.

Almost all of these workers are employed by the Army, Air Force, and Navy at bases throughout the country.

Food service workers (WG7408) help feed the hungry. They prepare and serve meals and clean the kitchen and dining room. The lowest grade is WG-1. The Department of Veterans Affairs employs more than half the government's food service workers at hospitals all over the country; the Defense Department also employs many of these workers.

Forestry technicians and smoke jumpers (GS462) help manage the country's woodlands. Smoke jumpers are firefighters who parachute into areas where there are forest fires. They are seasonal employees who must meet strict physical requirements and be trained parachutists. Not surprisingly, the jobs are few.

Forestry technicians collect data, take measurements, maintain equipment, look for signs of disease, and help with fire-control activities. Applicants can qualify for the lowest grade (GS-4) if they have had two years of experience in forestry, farming, soil conservation, or similar work. Two years of education after high school can also qualify applicants for GS-4 positions. The Forest Service of the Department of Agriculture employs 90 percent of all forestry technicians, few of whom work in Washington.

Heavy mobile equipment mechanics (WG5803) fix bulldozers, combat tanks, and other heavy duty vehicles. The qualifications are similar to those for an auto mechanic, with the addition of knowledge about hydraulic systems. WG-10 is the equivalent of a journey worker. Almost all 10,000 of these workers are employed by the Army, Navy, and Air Force.

Janitors or porters (WG3566; *custodial workers*) keep buildings clean. They collect wastepaper, vacuum rugs, wax floors, and mop hallways. The qualifications for the lowest grade (WG-1) are the ability to read signs, follow simple instructions, and use ordinary cleaning tools. The Army, Navy, Veterans Administration, and Department of Health and Human Services each employs over 1,000 janitors, as does the General Services Administration, the agency that owns or manages many of the government's buildings.

Laborers (WG3502) load and unload trucks, move material, clean the grounds surrounding buildings, collect garbage, and help skilled craft workers as directed. Workers are called "laborers," because the job is easily learned, rather than because it requires heavy work. Many of these jobs are not strenuous, although some require the constant lifting of sacks and boxes that weigh more than 100 pounds.

Laborers can usually learn their particular job in just a few days, so applicants frequently don't need any experience to qualify for the lowest grade (WG-1). More than half a dozen agencies employ at least a thousand laborers each, including the Army, the Navy, the Department of the Interior, and the Air Force.

Machinists (WG3414) make metal parts for machines. They read blueprints, set up their tools, and make the finished product. Their work must be very precise, since the measurement of the product may need to be correct within one one-thousandth of an inch. Two-thirds of the machinists employed by the government work for the Navy. The Air Force, Army, and Tennessee Valley Authority also employ a large number of these workers.

Mail and file clerks (GS305) are often grouped together, although they perform fairly different tasks. Mail clerks collect, route, and distribute letters, memos, publications, telegrams, and packages. File clerks classify material and organize it in an easily accessible manner.

Willingness to perform routine work is required of applicants for the lowest grade (GS-1). Applicants for the next higher grade must have a high school diploma and pass a written test. Although there are more than 23,000 workers employed in these positions throughout the government, the average grade is quite low, and the chances for advancement are not as good as those of secretaries or typists. The jobs are located all over the country.

Maintenance mechanics (WG4749) ensure that government vehicles keep moving. Major employers include the Army, the Department of Transportation, and the General Services Administration.

Medical technicians (GS600 series) assist physicians and other health care workers do their jobs. Naturally, the agencies with hospital systems, such as the Armed Forces and the Veterans Administration, are the major employers.

Motor vehicle operators (WG5703) drive cars, ambulances, trucks, and buses. They must know how to drive, read maps, and load cargo. The lowest grade is WG-5. The Army, Navy, Air Force, and Department of Veterans Affairs each employs over a thousand of these workers.

Nursing assistants (GS621) help registered nurses care for patients. Nursing assistants at lower grades (GS-1 and 2) are often called nursing aides or orderlies outside the government; at the next higher grades (GS-3 and above), they may be called licensed practical nurses or licensed vocational nurses. Some people find the work unpleasant, since nursing assistants take care of such basic needs as bathing and feeding patients and emptying bedpans. But the job also offers the satisfaction of working directly with people. Nursing assistants take temperatures and blood pressure readings, assist in operating rooms by passing instruments and positioning patients, prepare patients for examinations, and set up equipment. At higher levels, the work is more complex.

No education or experience is needed for the lowest grade (GS-1). There is a test for GS-2 and 3, but it can be waived if the applicant has a high school education or is trained as a practical nurse.

Almost 35,000 nursing assistants work for the federal government, 30,000 of them in hospitals run by the *Department of Veterans Affairs*. Any local federal hospital can provide further information about employment.

Personnel clerks and assistants (GS203) do the clerical and technical work that must be done so that the government can hire people. They may also be called staffing clerks or specialists, classification clerks or specialists, employee development clerks or specialists, or employee relations clerks or specialists. They check the forms that applicants fill out, maintain lists of applicants who are eligible for a job, prepare reports, and provide basic information about personnel regulations. The assistants specialize more than the clerks, either assisting a personnel specialist or working independently.

Clerks begin at the GS-4 level, which requires a year of general office experience and a year's experience in a job that involved a knowledge of personnel practices. Assistants start at GS-5. Applicants need one year of general and two years of specialized experience to qualify as assistants. A college degree qualifies applicants for GS-5 if they have majored in subjects such as statistics, the social sciences, journalism, public administration, personnel administration, industrial relations, or management analysis. About half these workers are employed by the Departments of Defense and Agriculture.

Pipefitters (WG4205) install pipes used to carry air, water, oil, gas, and other materials from one location to another. The pipes have to be bent, cut, and threaded so they fit tightly together and don't leak. Pipe-fitters must be able to read blueprints and plan the layout for a system of pipes. The Navy employs half the pipefitters in the government.

Reporting stenographers, shorthand reporters, and *clerk stenographers* (GS312) make records of conferences, hearings, interviews, and speeches. They take notes, which need not be word-for-word, either in shorthand or with a shorthand writing machine. Reporting stenographers must be able to record 120 words per minute. Shorthand reporters make word-for-word records of conferences and meetings. They must be able to take dictation at 160 words per minute for the lowest grade (GS-6) and 175 words per minute for all higher grades. *There is no experience or particular training required for entry-level positions in either occupation.* The Departments of the Army and the Air Force each employ over 1,000 of these workers.

Secretaries (GS318) in government, like infantry soldiers in the Army, are indispensable. They work in almost every office. Their duties include answering letters, maintaining records and files, making travel arrangements for other staff members, keeping track of their supervisor's appointments, and usually, though not always, typing. The lowest grade for a secretary is GS-3; the highest is GS-11. The grade of a particular secretary's position depends on the grade of the supervisor.

Secretaries must have a high school diploma and one additional year of education or clerical experience. They must also be poised, neat, discrete, and able to work alone and with others. These qualities cannot be tested, so the Office of Personnel Management recommends that would-be secretaries be hired first as clerk-typists. Clerk-typists who have the appropriate personal characteristics can then be placed in secretarial jobs.

The demand for secretaries has been great for many years and is likely to remain so. All the large agencies employ at least 1,000. The total number employed exceeds 80,900.

Secretaries have a chance to advance into professional and administrative positions if they take advantage of government training programs. Advancement is not easy and sometimes requires being in the right position at the right time, but it is possible.

Sheet metal mechanics (WG3806) or sheet metal workers make the ducts through which air moves from one part of a building to another, repair tin roofs, and make all kinds of flat metal objects. They cut the metal with power saws or hand shears and then rivet or weld it together.

Almost all 13,300 of these workers are employed by the Defense Department.

Shorthand reporters: See Reporting Stenographers in this chapter.

Supply clerks and technicians (GS2005) prepare orders, keep records, update inventories, and perform the many other tasks necessary to make sure that government employees have the materials they need to do their jobs. The work can be fairly routine at lower levels, but it requires the mastery of complicated regulations and procedures at higher levels. Applicants must usually pass a written test to qualify. To qualify for GS-4, applicants must also have (a) one year of general clerical experience and one year of experience as a supply clerk; (b) two years of experience as a supply clerk; or (c) two years of education after high school. The Department of Defense and the Veterans Administration are the largest employers of these 31,500 workers.

Typists: See Clerk-Typists in this chapter.

Warehouse workers (WG6907) unload trucks, move material around the warehouse, and keep records of what was shipped and received. More than 24,800 people hold these jobs, mostly with the Department of Defense and the Department of Veterans Affairs.

OTHER OCCUPATIONS

In addition to the occupations described above, there are many other clerical, technical, and blue-collar occupations offered by the federal government. The following occupations employ 5,000 to 10,000 workers.

Air conditioning equipment mechanic WG5306
Aircraft engine mechanic WG8602
Automotive mechanic WG5823
Biological technician GS404
Carpenter WG4607
Computer clerk and assistant GS335
Education and training technician GS1702
Electrician, high voltage WG2810
Equipment specialist GS1670
Food inspector GS1863

Guard GS085
Industrial equipment mechanic WG5352
Legal clerk and technician GS986
Medical clerk GS679
Military personnel clerk and technician GS204
Miscellaneous transportation/mobile equipment maintenance worker
    WG5801
Painting WG4102
Police GS083
Procurement clerk and assistant GS1106
Production controller GS1152
Purchasing agent GS1105
Welder WG3703

CHAPTER 7

THE EXECUTIVE AGENCIES

JOB LOCATIONS

Every county in the United States has at least one federal employee—at the post office, if nowhere else. Federal employees also live and work in 150 foreign countries. the largest concentration of government jobs, however, is in Washington. But to give an accurate and complete account of where the jobs are, you would have to have a specific job in mind, because the kinds of jobs found in Washington, D.C., are not the same as the jobs found in Paris, Kentucky, or Paris, France.

The Office of Personnel Management says—truthfully—that only about 15 percent of all federal white-collar workers are employed in Washington. It is also true, however, that the percentage of professionals working in the nation's capital is much higher than elsewhere. The message is simple: You can work for the government just about anywhere. But the more important the job, in terms of its impact on the way the government operates, the more likely the job is to be in Washington.

On the other hand, the more direct influence a job has on an individual citizen, the more likely it is that the job will be located far away from the huge buildings within sight of the Washington Monument. For example, most of the people who set the general qualifications for federal jobs work in the capital. But when you apply for a job in Missouri, the person who determines if *you* are qualified works in Kansas City.

If you plan a career with the federal government, you will probably spend some time in Washington, planning and administering programs, and some time "in the field" (as the rest of the country is called) putting those programs into action. The kind of program you work on will depend upon the agency for which you work.

The first—and longest—part of this chapter describes many of the executive agencies, so you will have some idea if that agency's responsibilities appeal to you. Next, three cities in Texas serve to illustrate the kinds of jobs found in regional headquarters like Dallas, large cities like Houston, and small cities like Big Springs. The jobs available around the world are discussed last.

The federal government has fewer agencies than there are lakes in Minnesota, but it has enough so that counting them is no easy matter. Commissions and boards pass in and out of existence, combine and split off, with regularity. A few years ago, there was no Department of Education. Now there is. Tomorrow it might be gone. Suffice it to say that there are more than 100 agencies, from ACTION to the Department of Veterans Affairs.

In the following pages, many of the largest of these agencies are described. Besides describing the agency's function, the entry indicates its major occupations and major divisions. Sources of employment information are also given. The addresses and phone numbers presented here are usually of the national headquarters of each agency or division; almost every one of the agencies has other offices around the country.

The agencies are listed here in alphabetical order for ease of reference, but a job hunter should be more concerned with their size. Obviously, the larger agencies offer many more opportunities than do the smaller ones. The agencies covered in this chapter include the Army, Navy, Department of Veterans Affairs, Air Force, Health and Human Services, Treasury, Agriculture, Interior, Transportation, Justice, Commerce, Labor, Tennessee Valley Authority, National Aeronautics and Space Administration, General Services Administration, Energy, Housing and Urban Development, State, Environmental Protection Agency, Education, Office of Personnel Management, International Communications Agency, and Small Business Administration. The Postal Service is discussed in the next chapter and the Congressional Branch is discussed in Chapter 9.

ACTION

ACTION serves as an umbrella under which several agencies staffed primarily by volunteers gather. The *Peace Corps,* once its best known component, was made a separate agency in 1981; it is described later in this chapter. ACTION now has four major components: *VISTA (volunteers in Service to America),* the *Foster Grandparents Program, Retired Senior Volunteer Program,* and the *Senior Companion Program.*

Not all the jobs with ACTION are for volunteers. It employs about 1,4000 paid workers in a wide variety of white-collar occupations. Information on employment can be obtained from ACTION, Personnel Management Division, 1100 Vermont Ave., NW, Washington, D.C. 20525; (202) 634-9263. Information on volunteering can be obtained from the ACTION office in each state.

AGRICULTURE

The *Department of Agriculture (USDA)* illustrates the complexity of modern government in general and the federal government in particular. It now employs about 117,00 people. That's many more than it employed at the turn of the century, yet the number of farms has decreased since then. The number of employees has gone up because agriculture is a far more complicated business than it was in 1900 and because the responsibilities of the Department have grown.

The following occupations each have at least 1,000 workers: accountant, agricultural commodity grader, agricultural management specialist, biological technician, civil engineer, clerk-typist, food inspection technician, forester, forestry technician, loan specialist, plant protection and quarantine officer, secretary, soil conservation officer, soil scientist, and veterinarian. The Department's central employment office is located in Room 1080, South Building, Washington, D.C. 20250; (202) 447-5626.

The Department has seven main divisions, each of which has major subdivisions of its own: *Small Community and Rural Development, Marketing and Inspection Services, Food and Consumer Services,*

International Affairs and Commodity Programs, Science and Education, Natural Resources and Environment, and *Economics.*

AGRICULTURE SUBDIVISIONS

Small Community and Rural Development

Principal components within *Small Community and Rural Development* include the *Farmers Home Administration,* the *Rural Electrification Administration,* and the *Federal Crop Insurance Corporation.*

The Farmers Home Administration lends money to people who wish to own family farms or need to make improvements on farms they already own. It employs agricultural management specialists who determine whether the purpose of a particular loan request warrants granting the loan. Although headquartered in Washington, D.C., the agency carries on much of its work at the local level. It has 2,200 county offices, usually located in the county seat, spread through all 50 states, Puerto Rico, and the Virgin Islands. Information on employment is available from the Director, Personnel Division, Farmers Home Administration, USDA, Washington, D.C. 20250; (202) 447-4323.

The *Federal Crop Insurance Corporation* does what its name says: It sells farmers insurance against the loss of crops caused by bad weather, disease, or insect plagues. It employs people like crop insurance specialists, who sell the insurance and inspect damaged crops to determine the amount of the loss, and underwriters, who set the insurance premiums. Insurance is offered—and jobs are available—in all 50 states. Information is available about employment from the Personnel Office, Federal Crop Insurance Corporation, USDA, Washington, D.C. 20250; (202) 447-6795.

Marketing and Inspection Services

Marketing and Inspections Services comprise the Agricultural Cooperative Service, the Agricultural Marketing Service, the Animal and Plant Health Inspection Service, the Federal Grain Inspection Service, the Food Safety and Inspection Service, the Office of Transportation, and the Packers and Stockyards Administration.

The *Animal and Plant Inspection Service* employs about 14,000 people throughout the world. This agency is responsible for controlling pests and diseases that threaten the country's plants and farm animals. Its employees must be able to identify diseased animals and plants and control the outbreak, imposing a quarantine if necessary. To perform their jobs efficiently, officials are stationed throughout the country carrying on inspection and eradication programs. Quarantine inspection officers work at all major ocean, Great Lakes, air and border ports of entry in the continental United States, Hawaii, Alaska, Puerto Rico, the Virgin Islands, the Bahamas, and Bermuda. In addition, inspectors in the Netherlands, Belgium, Germany, Italy, France, and Japan supervise the certification of flower bulbs being shipped to this country. There are also officials in Mexico who supervise the fumigation of fruit before it is sent north. Employees of the Veterinary Service Program—the Animal part of the Animal and Plant Inspection Service—not only look for signs of disease in animals on farms and ranches, but also inspect animals being imported, and administer federal laws for the humane handling of animals that cross state borders, including the elephants in the circus and the puppies at the pet store. The Animal and Plant Inspection Service hires specialists in many scientific fields, such as veterinary medicine, botany, and plant pathology. Information about employment can be obtained from the Personnel Division, Field Servicing Office, Animal and Plant Inspection Service, USDA, 100 North 6th St., Butler Sq. West, Minneapolis, Minn. 55403; (612) 370-2227.

The *Food Safety and Inspection Service* touches the life of every American. It is responsible for the stamps you see on meat and poultry: *"Inspected USDA."* Its employees set standards of quality for more than 300 agricultural products. They enforce the standards by inspecting animals when they are slaughtered and food when it is processed.

Other agencies within Marketing Services are responsible for ensuring that farmers are charged reasonable freight rates, protecting the rights of persons who develop new varieties of plants, ensuring that different kinds of grain meet official standards, and inspecting stockyards. An indication of the challenge facing the Department of Agriculture can be seen from its responsibility in administering the *Packers and*

Stockyards Act of 1921. This job alone entails the supervision of 2,000 public stockyards, 3,000 private livestock buying yards, 5,500 meatpackers, 15,000 livestock commission firms and dealers, and 400 poultry dealers and processors. No wonder the Department is bigger now than it was in 1900.

Information about each of the agencies within Marketing Services can be obtained from the Personnel Division, USDA, P.O. Box 96456, Washington, D.C. 20250; (202) 447-8999.

Food and Consumer Services

Just three agencies make up *Food and Consumer services:* the *Food and Nutrition Service,* the *Human Nutrition Information Service,* and the *Office of the Consumer Advisor.* The Food and Nutrition Service runs the *Food Stamp, School Lunch and Breakfast,* and *Supplemental Food Programs.* It employs home economists and specialists in management, finance, food distribution, and nutrition. It has regional offices in Atlanta, Chicago, Dallas, Princeton, and San Francisco, as well as branch offices in many cities and towns throughout the country. Information on employment is available from the Employment Branch, Personnel Division, Food and Nutrition Service, USDA, Alexandria, VA 22302; (703) 756-3276.

International Affairs and Commodity Programs

International Affairs and Commodity Programs include the Agricultural Stabilization and Conservation Service, the Commodity Credit Corporation, the Foreign Agricultural Service, and the Office of International Cooperation and Development.

Raising crops and animals is a boom-or-bust operation for many farmers; the programs administered by the *Agricultural Stabilization and Conservation Service* and the *Commodity Credit Corporation* are designed to help farmers weather disasters and prevent economic loss due to overproduction.

The *Foreign Agricultural Service* of the Department assigns agricultural attachés and secretaries to 65 posts throughout the world. The Department has more than 1,000 employees overseas. The Foreign

Agricultural Service primarily needs agricultural economists and secretaries, but it also recruits agricultural marketing specialists. Like the other agencies that employ people abroad, it prefers to transfer workers already employed by the government, rather than to risk sending an untested employee overseas.

Science and Education

Science and Education is made up of the Agricultural Research Service, the Cooperative State Research Service, the Extension Service, and the National Agricultural Library.

As you might guess, the *Agricultural Research Service* looks for ways to improve crops, livestock, soil, and overall farm production. It recruits agronomists, botanists, chemists, entomologists, geneticists, pathologists, physiologists, microbiologists, parasitologists, animal scientists, engineers, veterinarians, soil scientists, physicists, horticulturists, and nutritionists. Information about employment is available from regional offices in Peoria, Illinois; New Orleans; and Oakland, California; as well as from the Personnel Division, Agricultural Research Service, USDA, Beltsville, MD 20705; (301) 344-2264.

The policies of the *Extension Service* reach into almost every county in the country. Working through the land grant universities in each state and through the county governments, the Extension Service provides the public with expert advice through educational programs on gardening, farming, home economics, and related subject. You will find the Extension Service listed in local telephone directories under the name of your county.

Natural Resources and Environment

Natural Resources and Environment has only two components: the Forest Service and Soil Conservation Service.

The *Forest Service* is responsible for 191 million acres of federally owned woods and grasslands in 44 states, the Virgin Islands, and Puerto Rico. These areas are not simply a chain of parks and preserves. They are a national heritage which the Forest Service manages, so that they serve the purposes of recreation and conservation at the same time that they produce raw material for the lumber industry and provide forage for livestock. The Forest Service employs foresters, landscape architects, range conservationists, civil engineers, and wildlife biologists. Information about employment can be obtained from the Forest Service, USDA, P.O. Box 96090, Washington, D.C., 20090; (202) 447-3670. All Forest Service field offices also accept employment application.

The *Soil Conservation Service* works with state and local governments to develop ways to prevent the depletion of nutrients from the soil and other effects of poor soil management. Administrators, botanists, economists, engineers, farm managers, foresters, and many other specialists work for the Soil Conservation Service. Information about employment can be obtained from the Chief, Employment Branch, Personnel Division, Soil Conservation Service, USDA, P.O. Box 2890, Washington, D.C. 20013; (202) 447-4543.

AIR FORCE

The work of the Air Force needs little explanation: Its task, in collaboration with the other branches of the Armed Forces, is to defend the national and overseas interests of the United States. To perform this task, it employs several hundred thousand people—226,000 of whom are civilians—in over a thousand occupations. Since the machinery the Air Force uses is so complicated, it needs a wide range of engineers and scientists. Because of its size, it also employs a wide range of management specialists, accountants, management analysts, and attorneys, as well as procurement specialists, computer experts, nurses, and intelligence workers.

The following white-collar occupations employ over 1,000 workers each: accountant, aerospace engineer, budget analyst, clerk-typist, computer specialist, electronics engineer, fire protection worker, general engineer, inventory manager, production controller, secretary, and training instructor.

Blue-collar occupations with at least 1,000 workers include the following: air conditioning equipment mechanic, aircraft electronics system installer and repairer, aircraft engine mechanic, aircraft mechanic, aircraft ordinance systems mechanic, automotive mechanic, carpenter, electrician, electronic integrated system mechanic, electronics mechanic, food service worker, heavy mobile equipment mechanic, instrument mechanic, laborer, machinist, meatcutter, miscellaneous warehousing and stock handling worker, motor vehicle operator, painter, powered support systems mechanic, sheet metal mechanic, store worker, and warehouse worker.

Among the major commands and agencies within the Air Force are the Logistics Command, Audit Agency, Office of Special Investigations, Medical Services, Manpower and Personnel Center, Information and News Center, Inspection and Safety Center, Accounting and Finance Center, Operational Test and Evaluation Center, Engineering and Service Center, Intelligence Service, and Commissary Service.

Information about jobs at nearby bases can be obtained from the *civilian personnel office* of the base. Information about employment in the Washington area is available from the Directorate of Administration, U.S. Air Force, The Pentagon, Washington, D.C. 20330; (202) 545-6700.

ARMY

The Army is the biggest department in the federal government, employing 375,000 civilians in more than 1,200 occupations. For 17 groups of occupations, the Army has a career internship program that provides training and opportunities for promotion. These occupational groups are personnel administration, comptrollership, safety management, supply management, procurement, quality and reliability assurance, education and training, material maintenance, engineering and science, intelligence, ammunition surveillance, library science, information and editing, automatic data processing, communications management, manpower management, and transportation. college graduates are usually hired for these internships.

All the following occupations have at least 1,000 civilian workers in the Army: accountant, air conditioning equipment mechanic, aircraft mechanic, automotive mechanic, budget analyst, carpenter, civil engineer, clerk-typist, computer specialist, contract and procurement specialist, custodial worker, education and vocational training specialist, electrician, electronics engineer, electronics mechanic, engineering equipment operator, engineering technician, explosives operative, fire protection worker, food service worker, forklift operator, general engineer, general physical scientist, heavy mobile equipment mechanic, guard, inventory management specialist, laborer, lock and dam operator, maintenance mechanic, mechanical engineer, material sorting and classifying worker, machinist, miscellaneous transportation and mobile equipment mechanic, motor vehicle operator, nurse, packing worker, painter, quality assurance specialist, secretary, sheet-metal mechanic, store worker, supply management specialist, training instructor, warehouse worker, and welder.

Information about local opportunities can be obtained from the civilian personnel office of the Army installation where you wish to work. In addition, each of the agencies described below can provide employment information.

ARMY SUBDIVISIONS

Given its size, the Army naturally has very large subdivisions. Some of the larger ones are the Audit Agency, the Communications Command, the Corps of Engineers, the Finance and Accounting Center, the Army Forces Command, the Material Command, and the Medical Department.

The *Army Audit Agency* once did nothing more than check pay and property records, but times have changed. Now it performs sophisticated internal audits on every phase of the Army's operations to ensure that the taxpayers' money is well spent. A major employer of accountants and auditors, it has offices throughout this country and Europe. Considerable travel is often required. Further information about its training program for college graduates in auditing is available from the Personnel and Employment Service—Washington, Recruitment and Placement Branch, the Pentagon, Washington, D.C. 20310; (202) 545-6700.

The *Army Communications Command* builds and operates communications systems all over the world. It employs more than 30,000 people—civilian and military—who are experts with computers, communications satellites, all types of radio transmitters, automatic switching equipment, telephone lines, undersea cables, and electronic coding and decoding equipment. Employment information is available from the headquarters: U.S. Army Communications Command, Attn: CC-PA-CP, Fort Huachuca, Ariz. 85613; (602) 538-3030.

The *Army Corps of Engineers* does more to develop the country's water resources than any other government agency. It builds dams, reservoirs, levees, harbors, locks, and many other structures. It also manages the construction of family housing, office buildings, barracks, and other buildings for the Army. To do these jobs, the Army Corps employs about 40,000 civilians, nearly 9,000 of whom are engineers. The jobs are very widely scattered, the Corps having learned long ago that nothing makes a congressional representative approve an agency's budget faster than having a project in the home district. Further information is available from the Civilian Personnel Division, Army Corps of Engineers, 20 Massachusetts Ave., NW, Washington, D.C. 20314; (202) 272-0720.

Among other things, the *U.S. Army Finance and Accounting Center* keeps track of the pay due the Army's millions of soldiers. It hires people in administration, comptrollership, automatic data processing, and other specialties. All the jobs are in *Indianapolis,* where the Center is located. Information about employment is available from the Civilian Personnel Office, U.S. Army Finance and Accounting Center, Fort Benjamin Harrison, Indianapolis, Ind. 46249; (317) 542-2433.

The *U.S. Army Forces Command* is the largest component of the Army. Its head, a four-star general, commands all the soldiers in the United States. The kinds of jobs available in so large an organization number over 1,000 and include just about all the occupations described in this book. Information can be obtained from the civilian personnel office of any local army installation; from the regional headquarters at Fort George G. Meade, Md.; Fort Sam Houston, Tex.; the Presidio of San Francisco, Calif.; and from the national headquarters: Commander, U.S. Army Forces Command, Attn: AFPR-Cpt, Fort McPherson, Ga. 30330; (404) 752-3784.

The *Army Materiel Command* has over 115,000 civilian employees, which is more than most cabinet-level departments can claim. In addition to large numbers of clerical and administrative workers, it employs engineers, scientists, procurement and supply specialists, and computer experts. They work together to develop, test, buy, produce, store, distribute, maintain, and keep track of the thousands of different kinds of equipment the Army needs, from ration kits to tanks. For further information, contact the commanding General, U.S. Army Materiel Command, 200 Stovall St., Alexandria, VA 22333; (202) 325-2130.

The *Army Health Services Command* is part of the Medical Department. The largest single medical organization in the world, it operates hospitals and health programs for soldiers and their dependents at Army bases throughout this country and overseas. Professionals, technicians, and paraprofessionals in every health occupation are employed. For civilian professionals, information can be obtained from Health Services Command, Civilian Health Occupations Recruiting Office, Ft. Sam Houston, TX 78234; (512) 221-6630. For reserve and active duty positions with the Army Medical Department, contact AMDDDPERSA, Attn: Procurement Division, 1900 Half St. SW., Washington, D.C. 20324; (202) 693-6170.

CENTRAL INTELLIGENCE AGENCY

One of the country's principal gatherers of information crucial to the nation's security, the *Central Intelligence Agency* is cloaked in secrecy. Neither the amount of its budget nor the number of its employees are matters of public record. Naturally, however, it does have workers— about 25,000—and it does have a personnel office you can contact: Central Intelligence Agency, Office of Personnel, Washington, D.C. 20505; (703) 482-1100.

The CIA usually hires college graduates in economics, international trade, auditing, political science, international relations, history, physics, chemistry, electronics, medicine, and library science. Employees are not within the regular civil service system administered by the Office of Personnel Management, but their pay and other benefits are claimed to be similar to those received by most government workers. The CIA often does its own recruiting through college placement offices.

COMMERCE

The *Department of Commerce* and its 35,000 employees promote the growth of the nations's business and industries. Some agencies within the Department promote business directly. Examples of these are the *International Trade Administration,* and *Minority Business Development Agency.* Other agencies serve business by registering patents (the *Patent and Trademark Office)* and setting uniform standards (the *National Bureau of Standards).* Still other agencies gather the information businesses need to plan their activities; these include the *Bureau of Economic Analysis,* the *Bureau of the Census,* and the *National Oceanic and Atmospheric Administration* (formerly the National Weather Service). Finally, the *National Technical Information Service* runs a publishing operation that issues 70,000 titles a year.

The larger occupations in the Department include the following: attorney, cartographer, chemist, computer specialist, economist, electronics engineer, fishery biologist, meteorologist, patent examiner, secretary, statistician, and trade specialist. Information is available from the U.S. Department of Commerce, 14th and Constitution Ave., NW, Washington, D.C. 20230; (202) 377-2000.

The *International Trade Administration* tries to expand overseas markets for American goods by promoting products made in the United States and encouraging companies to enter foreign markets. It also serves as an advocate within the government for policies favorable to business. Employment information is available from the Personnel Office, Room 4808, Hoover Bldg., 14th St. and Constitution Ave. NW., Washington, D.C. 20230; (202) 377-3071.

The *Economic Development Administration* stimulates business in depressed localities by lending money and providing technical assistance to local businesses. The personnel office is in Room 7316, Hoover Bldg., 14th St. and Constitution Ave. NW., Washington, D.C. 20230; (202) 377-2000.

The *Patent and Trademark Office* issues 60,000 patents each year that give inventors—or their employers—the exclusive right to sell the fruits of their ingenuity and creativity. Before a patent can be issued, however, records of existing patents must be checked to make sure that the invention really is new. Information is available from the Office of

Personnel, Patent and Trademark Office CPK-1, Suite'700, Washington, D.C. 20231. A toll free number, (800) 368-3064, was set up to provide information for people interested in patent examiner positions.

The *National Bureau of Standards and Technology* tests consumer products, looks for ways to improve the country's technology, and sets the standards for weights and measures. It also runs some of the largest physics laboratories in the country at Gaithersburg, Md., and Boulder, Colo. More than half of its 3,000 workers are technicians or scientists. For information, contact the Personnel Division, Gaithersburg, MD 20899; (301) 975-2000.

The *Bureau of the Census* keeps count of the country's population and production. It hires statisticians galore to work at its headquarters in Suitland, Md. The address of the Personnel Division is Suitland, MD 20233.

The *National Oceanic and Atmospheric Administration* studies the oceans and runs the Weather Service. It hires cartographers, physicists, geodesists, engineers, meteorologists, and fishery biologists. For employment information, contact the Personnel Officer, National Oceanic and Atmospheric Administration, Room 716, 6010 Executive Blvd., Washington, D.C. 20852; (301) 443-8834.

DEFENSE

One out of every three civilians in the executive agencies works for the *Department of Defense*. In addition to the agencies described here, see the sections of this chapter on the Air Force, Army, and Navy to get a more complete picture of the kinds of workers employed by the department.

The *Defense Logistics Agency* provides supplies for the Armed Forces. It buys, stores, and distributes food, clothing, gasoline, electronics equipment, and more. Just under 49,000 civilians work for this agency. It hires experts in supply and inventory management, procurement, contract administration, and quality assurance, as well as in clerical and administrative specialties. Warehouse workers, material sorting and classifying workers, and packing workers are also numerous. More than 90 percent of the Agency's employees are with field offices located throughout the United States. Its headquarters, located across the Potomac River from Washington, can provide information about employment. Contact the Defense Logistics Agency, DLA Administrative Support Center, Cameron Station, Alexandria, VA 22304; (202) 274-6000.

Most United States citizens employed overseas started working for their agency here at home. The *Department of Defense Dependents' Schools* is one agency that cannot recruit from its home-based staff, because it has none. The school system employs about 7,4000 teachers to instruct the children of military and civilian personnel stationed abroad. It recruits teachers and other education specialists who have had at least two years of active work experience within the last five years and meet other requirements. More information about the positions available in these schools can be obtained from the Chief, Teacher Recruitment, 2461 Eisenhower Avenue, Hoffman Bldg. I, Alexandria, VA 22331; (202) 325-0885.

The *Defense Mapping Agency* (DMA) employs about 7,000 civilians to make maps, nautical charts, and filmstrips for target positioning and missile directional systems. About half its employees are cartographers. Most positions are located in Washington or St. Louis, but there are smaller offices in several states and foreign countries. Employment inquiries should be sent to the Director, Personnel Office, at the following addresses: DMA Aerospace Center, St. Louis Air Force Station, MO 63118; (314) 263-4965. DMA Hydrographic/Topographic Center, 6500 Brookes Lane NW., Washington, D.C. 20315; (292) 227-2047. Executive/managerial applications should be addressed to Chief, Civilian Personnel Division, Headquarters, DMA, 8613 Lee Highway, Fairfax, VA 22031; (703) 285-9368.

The *Defense Contract Audit Agency* employs about 3,000 accountants and auditors whose job it is to evaluate the costs claimed by contractors, and review the efficiency of the contractors' operations. Agency headquarters are located near Washington, but more than 90 percent of its 3,500 employees are stationed in its 350 field offices in this country and abroad, or in one of the regional offices in Marietta, Ga., Waltham, Mass., Philadelphia, Chicago, Los Angeles, and San Francisco. Information is available from the Personnel Director, Defense Contract Audit Agency, Cameron Station, Alexandria, VA 22304; (202) 274-6875.

The *Defense Intelligence Agency* collects and distributes intelligence information. Not quite half its 2,300 employees are intelligence specialists; most of the rest are general administrative and clerical workers. For employment information, contact the Defense Intelligence Agency, Washington, D.C. 20340; (202) 695-7353.

The *Defense Investigative Service* conducts security investigations of Defense Department personnel. It has 2,000 employees, about half of whom are investigators. For more information, contact the Assistant Director for Personnel and Security, Defense Investigative Service, 1900 Half St. SW., Washington, D.C. 20324; (202) 475-0966.

The *Defense Communications Agency,* with 1,500 workers, operates a worldwide system of communications for intelligence gathering, weather reporting, administration, and other purposes. One of its field organizations is the *White House Communications Agency,* which makes sure that the President is always in touch with the major centers of the government. It employs electronics engineers, computer specialists, operations specialists, and administrative, clerical, and technical workers. Information about employment can be obtained from the Civilian Personnel Division (Code 306), Headquarters, Defense Communications Agency, Washington, D.C. 20305; (202) 692-9012. The street address is 8th St. and South Courthouse Rd., Arlington, VA 22204.

EDUCATION

The *Department of Education* only became a separate cabinet level department in 1979. Political winds blew it into existence, and a change in the weather may return its functions to another department. Regardless, the programs it administers will probably continue, and the Department itself—no matter where it appears on the organization charts—will still employ 5,000 or so workers. The Department conducts a wide range of programs designed to improve elementary, secondary, and higher education—especially for the disadvantaged. Besides working with institutions and agencies of state and local governments, it runs programs that aid students directly, such as *Basic Education Opportunity Grants* and the *Guaranteed Student Loan Program.* Educational specialist and civil rights analyst are the largest occupations in the Department. *There is a single source of employment information,* the Office of Personnel, 400 Maryland Ave. SW., Washington, D.C. 20202; (202) 708-5366.

ENERGY

The *Department of Energy* is responsible for research into new sources of energy, the regulation of energy production, and oddly enough, the nuclear weapons program. The Department was created by bringing together existing agencies, such as the Energy Research and Development Administration, the Federal Power Commission, and the Bonneville Power Administration, which is basically a hydro-electric company. It employs 16,300 people in a wide range of clerical, administrative, and blue-collar positions, notably secretary, accountant, general engineer, electrical engineer, and attorney. Form more information, contact the Personnel Office, Department of Energy, 1000 Independence Ave. SW., Washington, D.C. 20585; (202) 586-5000.

ENVIRONMENTAL PROTECTION AGENCY

The *Environmental Protection Agency* is both regulatory and research-oriented. As a regulatory agency, it sets and enforces standards such as those in the *Toxic Substances Control Act.* As a research organization, it strives to discover ways of improving our natural surroundings. Both its functions aim at the reduction of air, water, and soil pollution. Among its 15,000 employees are environmental specialists, environmental engineers, general physical scientists, chemists, biologists, medical doctors, lawyers, and secretaries. Employment information is available from the Personnel Management Division, Gallery 1, West Tower, 401 M St. SW., Washington, D.C. 20460; (202) 382-2090.

EQUAL EMPLOYMENT OPPORTUNITY COMMISSION

The laws of the United States *forbid job discrimination based on race, color, creed, or national ancestry.* The *Equal Employment Opportunity Commission* and its 3,200 employees enforce these laws. Its employees (1,400 of whom are civil rights analysts, and almost 500 of whom are lawyers) investigate complaints and negotiate settlements. It has offices in 40 cities, including Washington, where the headquarters is located. In addition to the usual staff of clerical and administrative employees, the Commission hires lawyers and equal opportunity specialists. More information can be obtained from the Equal Employment Opportunity Commission, Personnel Office, 1801 L St., NW, Washington, D.C. 20507; (202) 663-4900.

FEDERAL COMMUNICATIONS COMMISSION

The airways through which radio and TV broadcasts travel are public property, and it is the responsibility of the *Federal Communications Commission* to see that our property is not misused. It has jurisdiction over AM and FM radio stations, television networks, cable television companies, and *even ham radio operators.* The FCC employs lawyers, electronics engineers, economists, accountants, administrators, computer specialists, and clerical personnel, about 2,000 people altogether. Most of the entry-level positions are located in the Washington headquarters, but much of the investigative and enforcement work is done at 40 different field offices and monitoring stations located throughout the country. Requests for employment information can be sent to the Chief, Staffing and Employment Services Branch, Personnel Management Division, Federal Communications Commission, 1919 M St. NW., Washington, D.C. 20554; (202) 632-7000.

FEDERAL DEPOSIT INSURANCE CORPORATION

When the Great Depression struck in 1929, many banks went broke. They lost the money they had invested, and the people who had deposited their savings in those banks were simply out of luck—or money. The *Federal Deposit Insurance Corporation (FDIC)* was set up to prevent such losses from recurring. It guarantees depositors of member banks—and 97 percent of all banks are members—that they will get their money back if the bank fails. To make sure the money is safe, the corporation regularly examines all member banks. Due to the banking problems that surfaced after federal deregulation of the banks in the 1980s, the FDIC has grown more rapidly than any other federal agency. From 1980–1989, the FDIC grew by almost 150 percent, jumping from about 3,500 workers in 1980 to almost 9,000 in 1989. It employs several thousand bank examiners. Examiners start as trainees; they are usually college graduates who majored in accounting, business administration, finance, or economics. Examiners travel extensively. Information on these and 1,400 other jobs is available from the Director, Office of Personnel Management, Federal Deposit Insurance Corporation, 550 17th St. NW., Washington, D.C. 20429; (202) 393-8400.

FEDERAL EMERGENCY MANAGEMENT AGENCY

The *Federal Emergency Management Agency* coordinates the preparation for and response to emergencies such as floods and nuclear war. Relatively small, it has only about 2,700 employees in various administrative, clerical, and engineering positions, most of which are located in Washington. Information on employment can be obtained from the Office of Personnel, Resource Management and Administration Directorate, 500 C St. SW., Washington, D.C. 20472; (202) 646-4600.

FEDERAL TRADE COMMISSION

The *Federal Trade Commission* is the government's consumer protection service. Its 1,000 workers administer such laws as the "Truth in Lending" legislation and enforce antitrust laws. Among its employees are the usual administration and clerical workers, 100 economists, and 500 lawyers. For information about employment, write the Director of

Personnel, Federal Trade Commission, Room 151, 6th St. and Pennsylvania Ave. NW., Washington, D.C. 20580; (202) 326-2222.

GENERAL SERVICES ADMINISTRATION

The *General Services Administration* is a conglomerate with 21,000 employees. Among the larger occupations are accountant, archivist, clerk-typist, contract and procurement specialist, general engineer, inventory management specialist, mechanical engineer, miscellaneous administration, police officer, property disposal specialist, quality assurance specialist, realty appraiser, secretary, and transportation specialist. In the late 1970s, the General Services Administration employed almost 40,000 workers, but personnel cuts during the Reagan years reduced this number by almost 50 percent.

The work of each major division is largely unrelated to the work of the others. For example, different agencies within the Administration run Federal Information Centers, build government office buildings, and maintain the memorial libraries for former Presidents. Its five divisions are the Public Buildings Service, Office of Federal Supply and Services, National Archives and Records Service, Office of Information Resource Management, and Federal Property Resources Service. The address of the central office is Personnel Office, General Services Administration, Room 1100, 18th and F Sts. NW., Washington, D.C. 20405; (202) 708-5082. However, applications are not kept on file; they are accepted only for announced vacancies. Furthermore, hiring is highly decentralized, much of it occurring in the regions.

The *Public Buildings Service* owns or leases more than 7,000 buildings. Its responsibility begins when the decision to erect a new building is made and doesn't end until the building is no longer needed by the government. Among the employees of the Service are engineers, architects, and property management and disposal specialists, as well as a large number of guards and building maintenance workers. Information about local employment is available at local government office buildings.

Federal Supply and Services (often referred to as the Federal Supply Service) spends an estimated $3,000,000,000 a year to provide government workers with the materials they need to do their jobs. It is a major employer of procurement specialists and other workers in supply-related occupations. For information about employment, contact Federal Supply and Services, Office of Personnel, Washington, D.C. 20406; (703) 557-8667.

The *Information Resources Management Service* runs the Federal Data Processing Center, Automatic Data Processing Procurement Programs, the government's telephone system, and the Federal Information Centers. Engineers, computer programmers, and telecommunications experts are among the people it hires. Information about employment can be obtained from the regional offices of the General Services Administration.

The *Federal Property Resources Service* manages the National Defense Stockpile of Strategic and Critical Materials and sells off real estate for which it can't find a use. For employment information, contact the regional offices of the General Services Administration.

HEALTH AND HUMAN SERVICES

The *Department of Health and Human Services,* with 126,400 workers, is among the biggest government agencies outside the Defense Department and the Postal Service. It employs more than 1,000 workers in each of the following occupations: accountant, chemist, computer specialist, consumer safety officer, contact representative, medical officer, nurse, program analyst, public health program specialist, secretary, social insurance claims examiner, social insurance representative and administrator, and social science analyst. As its name indicates, however, its functions fall into two distinct categories: *Health (the Public Health Service)* and *Human Services (the Social Security Administration).* It also operates an *Office of Human Development Services,* a *Health Care Financing Administration,* an *Office of Child Support Enforcement,* and other agencies.

The *Public Health Service* goes back to 1798, when hospitals were set up for America's merchant sailors. Running hospitals is still one of its functions, but it has many others as well. Among the major agencies with the Public Health Service are the *Health Resources and Services*

Administration, the *Centers for Disease Control,* the *National Institutes of Health,* the *Food and Drug Administration,* and the *Alcohol, Drug Abuse, and Mental Health Administration.*

The *Health Resources and Services Administration* provides direct medical care in communities and on Indian reservations that are not served by private or local government hospitals. It employs physicians, nurses, and many other health care professionals who are members of the Commissioned Corps of the Public Health Service. For information on medical, scientific, and technical positions, contact the Commissioned Personnel Operations Division, Room 4-35, Parklawn Bldg., 5600 Fishers Lane, Rockville, MD 20857; (301) 443-2086.

The *Centers for Disease Control* plan nationwide programs designed to eliminate or control communicable diseases. Its staff includes many doctors, scientists, and technicians. More information about employment in most occupations is available from the headquarters in Atlanta. Contact Recruitment and Placement, Room 1055, Centers for Disease Control, 1600 Clifton Road NE., Atlanta, GA 30333; (404) 329-3615. As with the Public Health Service, many medical, scientific, and technical workers are members of the Commissioned Corps of the Public Health Service. The address for information about the Corps is given in the previous paragraph.

The *National Institutes of Health* is a collection of a dozen institutes, such as the National Cancer Institute and the National Heart, Lung, and Blood Institute. The Institutes are responsible for health education and medical research. They run their own laboratories and also administer grants to universities and medical schools. The highly trained staff of the Institutes includes physicians, scientists, and medical engineers. Further information can be obtained from the Division of Personnel Management, NIH, Bethesda, MD 20892; (301) 496-4000. Like the Public Health Service, the National Institutes of Health has a Commissioned Officer Program. Information on this program is available from the Division of Personnel in Bethesda; ask for a copy of "Associate Training Programs in the Medical and Biological Sciences."

The *Food and Drug Administration* is a regulatory agency that sets quality standards for medicines, cosmetics, food, and medical devices. It employs consumer safety officers, pharmacologists, microbiologists, physiologists, chemists, statisticians, animal caretakers, and many other workers. Employment information for local areas is available at the thirty *Food and Drug Administration Consumer Affairs* offices located around the country; for information about work at the headquarters, contact the Personnel Office (HFA-400), Food and Drug Administration, 5600 Fishers Lane, Attn: Personnel, Room 4B18, Rockville, MD 20857; (301) 443-1544.

The *Social Security Administration* runs the largest pension fund in the world. To function efficiently, it has a 70,000 person army of claims authorizers, benefit examiners, economists, social insurance representatives, statisticians, and computer specialists. The agency has over 1,300 offices throughout the country, any of which can provide employment information. Or you can contact the national headquarters: Office of Human Resources, Social Security Administration, 6401 Security Blvd., Baltimore, MD 21235; (301) 965-1234.

HOUSING AND URBAN DEVELOPMENT

The *Department of Housing and Urban Development* administers programs that encourage the improvement of housing and the planned growth of towns and cities. It has field offices in many cities, and the majority of its 15,000 workers are located in the field offices. Construction analyst, loan specialist, and appraiser are among the larger occupations in the Department. Information on employment is available from the personnel divisions of the regional offices and from the Headquarters Office of Personnel, U.S. Department of Housing and Urban Development, 451 7th St. SW., Washington, D.C. 20410; (202) 708-1422.

INTERIOR

The *Department of the Interior,* the nation's principal conservation agency, is responsible for most of the public lands owned by the federal government. It controls more than 500 million acres, an area twice the size of Texas. It conducts land surveys, manages the national parks, protects wildlife, and is the government's official agency for Indian affairs. The

Department's 75,000 employees work in occupations such as the following: cartographer, civil engineer, clerk-typist, computer specialist, education and training specialist, education and training technician, fishery biologist, forester, general biologist, geologist, hydrologist, maintenance mechanic, park manager and park ranger, police officer, range conservationist, realty appraiser, secretary, and wildlife biologist.

The Department has many major components, such as the Bureau of Indian Affairs, the Fish and Wildlife Service, the Geological Survey, and the National Park Service.

The *Bureau of Indian Affairs* has the responsibility of encouraging Indians and native Alaskans to develop their full potential. To this end, it operates schools, provides technical assistance, and subsidizes projects like the construction of roads. Indian applicants receive preference in appointments. Information on employment can be obtained from the area personnel offices of the Bureau.

The *Fish and Wildlife Service* operates fish hatcheries and wildlife refuges and regulates the hunting of migratory birds. Employment information is available from regional offices in Atlanta; Albuquerque; Anchorage; Denver; Portland, Oregon; Newton Corner, Massachusetts; and Twin Cities, Minnesota. The address of the Office of Personnel at the Washington Headquarters is Room 3454, 18th and C Sts. NW., Washington, D.C. 20240; (202) 343-6104.

The *Geological Survey* systematically maps the United States and identifies areas likely to be rich in minerals, oil, and gas. Employment information can be obtained from the Recruitment and Placement Office, 215 National Center, 12201 Sunrise Valley Drive, Reston, VA 22092; (703) 860-6127.

The *National Park Service* manages national parks, monuments, historic sites, and recreational areas—about 330 different places that range in size from a small stone house to Yellowstone National Park. Its employees develop and maintain these areas and conduct educational programs. Information on employment is available from the Personnel Office, National Park Service, U.S. Department of the Interior, 18th and C Sts., NW, Washington, D.C. 20013; (202) 343-4648. Applications for seasonal (summer) employment should be sent to the regional offices in Boston, Philadelphia, Atlanta, Omaha, Denver, San Francisco, Seattle, and Washington. These offices, including the Washington office, will have information only about jobs in their respective regions.

INTERNATIONAL COMMUNICATIONS AGENCY

The *International Communications Agency,* formerly called the United States Information Agency, runs informational and cultural programs designed to promote greater understanding of the United States. It has its own Foreign Service made up of more than 1,000 foreign service information officers. The Agency, which has a total employment of 3,800, also hires secretaries, foreign affairs analysts, writers, electronics technicians, audio-visual production specialists, and other workers. For information on all these positions, contact the Recruitment and Examining Division, International Communications Agency, 301 4th St. SW., Washington, D.C. 20547; (202) 485-2618.

INTERSTATE COMMERCE COMMISSION

The first article of the Constitution gives the federal government the duty of regulating commerce between the states. The *Interstate Commerce Commission* is one of the agencies that carries out that duty. Trains, trucks, buses, barges, and pipelines that cross state lines are regulated by the Commission, one of the oldest of the regulatory agencies. Its major task is making sure that the rates companies charge are fair to both the receiver of the goods and the shipping company. At its headquarters in Washington, and at 56 field offices around the country, it employs 1,000 workers, including lawyers, transportation specialists, accountants, and auditors. For more information, contact the Director of Personnel, Room 1136, Interstate Commerce Commission, 12th St. and Constitution Ave. NW., Washington, D.C. 20423; (202) 275-7119.

JUSTICE

The largest law firm in the country, the *Department of Justice* provides legal advice to the President and to government agencies, represents the United States in court cases, and investigates possible violations of federal law. Among its 80,000 employees are lawyers, criminal investigators, accountants, immigration inspectors, chemists, computer specialists, border patrol agents, correctional officers, and teachers. Its major divisions are the Federal Bureau of Investigation, the Immigration and Naturalization Service, and the Bureau of Prisons, though there are many others.

The *Federal Bureau of Investigation* (FBI) looks for evidence that a crime has been committed. Besides its special agents, the Bureau employs fingerprint specialists and many other workers in administrative and clerical positions. For information, contact any field office, resident agency, or the Applicant Recruiting Office, FBI, 10th and Pennsylvania Ave., SW., Washington, D.C. 20520; (202) 514-2000.

The *Immigration and Naturalization Service* administers the country's immigration laws. Its border patrol is responsible for the 6,000 miles of border between this country and Canada and Mexico. Employment information is available from any regional or district office or from the Central Office, Immigration and Naturalization Service, 1425 Eye St. NW., Washington, D.C. 20546.

The *Bureau of Prisons* runs 45 federal penitentiaries and other correctional institutions. Medical personnel, such as physicians' assistants, are among the people employed in the prisons, in addition to the correctional officers. You can obtain information about jobs from any regional or field office or from the Central Office, Bureau of Prisons, 320 1st St. NW., Washington, D.C. 20534; (202) 724-3072.

Among the other divisions of the Department of Justice are the Antitrust Division, Civil Division, Civil Rights Division, Drug Enforcement Administration, Tax Division, and U.S. Marshals Service, each of which has its own personnel office.

Lawyers should make inquiries to the Director, Office of Attorney Personnel Management, Room 4311, U.S. Department of Justice, 10th St. and Constitution Ave. NW., Washington, D.C. 20530; (202) 633-3396.

LABOR

One of the smaller cabinet-level agencies, the Department of Labor and its 18,000 workers promote the welfare of wage earners and analyze information about the economy and the labor force. Among its major divisions are the *Employment and Training Administration, Employment Standards Administration, Occupational Safety and Health Administration,* and *Bureau of Labor Statistics.* Its largest occupations are computer specialist, economist, general attorney, industrial hygienist, manpower development specialist, mine safety specialist, safety management specialist, wage and hour compliance specialist, and worker compensation claims examiner. Employment information is available from eight different personnel offices for the various divisions within the department, from the regional offices, and from the Reception and Correspondence Unit, Room C5516, U.S. Department of Labor, 200 Constitution Ave. NW., Washington, D.C. 20210; (202) 523-6677.

NATIONAL AERONAUTICS AND SPACE ADMINISTRATION

NASA, the National Aeronautics and Space Administration, ran one of the nation's most spectacularly successful programs, culminating in the Apollo moon landing. While its recent projects have not been quite as heart-stopping, NASA continues its aeronautics and space research, employing over 21,000 persons—10,000 of whom are engineers, 1,500 of whom are secretaries, 1,400 of whom are scientists, 700 of whom are mathematicians, and the rest of whom are clerical and administrative workers. Inquiries concerning employment can be sent to the Director of Headquarters Personnel, NASA Headquarters, Washington, D.C. 20546; (202) 453-8480. That office will also provide a list of the field offices, which have local information.

NATIONAL LABOR RELATIONS BOARD

The rights of workers to organize in unions are established by various laws. These laws are administered by the *National Labor Relations*

Board and its 2,600 workers. Among its employees are lawyers, labor management relations examiners, field examiners, and clerical and administrative personnel. It has more than 50 field offices around the country. Applications for field examiner and attorney positions can be sent to the Personnel Operations Section, National Labor Relations Board, 1717 Pennsylvania Ave. NW., Washington, D.C. 20570; (202) 254-9044.

NAVY

The Department of the Navy employs almost 135,000 blue-collar and more than 164,000 white-collar civilians. They do everything from serving food in mess halls to conducting advanced research into the nature of the ocean. Most of the occupations that are described in the two previous chapters can be found in the Navy. At least 1,000 people work for the Navy in the following white-collar occupations: accountant, aerospace engineer, civil engineer, clerk-typist, contract administrator, education and vocational training specialist, electrical engineer, electronics engineer, electronics technician, engineering technician, fire protection worker, general engineer, inventory management specialist, mathematician, mechanical engineer, naval architect, nuclear engineer, secretary, and supply program administrator. At least 1,000 blue-collar workers are in each of the following occupations: air conditioning equipment mechanic, aircraft electronic systems installer and repairer, aircraft engine mechanic, aircraft mechanic, automotive mechanic, boiler plant operating worker, boilermaker, carpenter, custodial worker, electrician, electronics mechanic, equipment cleaner, heavy mobile equipment mechanic, industrial equipment mechanic, instrument mechanic, insulating worker, laborer, machinist, maintenance mechanic, marine machinery mechanic, motor vehicle operator, ordinance equipment mechanic, painter, pipefitter, rigger, sheet metal mechanic, shipfitter, shipwright, tools and parts attending worker, warehouse worker, and welder.

Positions are very widely spread throughout the coastal states. For further information about jobs in the Washington area, write the Director, Naval Civilian Personnel Command, Capital Region, 801 North

Randolph St., Arlington, VA 22203; (202) 696-4567. Each of the Navy's numerous local installations can provide information about jobs at that facility.

When filling overseas jobs, the Navy rarely recruits outside its own body of employees. When it does, it is usually looking for engineers, scientists, skilled trade workers, accountants, and auditors. Information about Navy jobs overseas is available from the civilian personnel officer at the nearest Navy installation.

NUCLEAR REGULATORY COMMISSION

The safe use of nuclear energy is the responsibility of the 3,300 employees of the *Nuclear Regulatory Commission*. This agency licenses companies that want to build or operate nuclear reactors or use nuclear material in other ways. Among the major occupations in the agency are security administration officer, secretary, nuclear engineer, general engineer, lawyer, and health physicist. *The agency is not in the regular civil service system and the Office of Personnel Management cannot give any advice about employment. Instead, contact the Director, Division of Organization and Personnel, Nuclear Regulatory Commission,* Washington, D.C. 20555; (301) 492-9027.

OFFICE OF PERSONNEL MANAGEMENT

The *Office of Personnel Management* is the government's principal personnel office. Although your first contact with it is likely to concern employment, most of its 6,000 workers deal with other matters, such as position descriptions, pensions, and health benefit plans. It employs personnel specialists, computer specialists, civil service retirement claims examiners, general claims examiners, and general investigators. For information about employment, contact the nearest *Federal Job Information Center.*

PEACE CORPS

More than 6,000 Peace Corps volunteers are currently serving in 70 countries around the world, trying to promote peace and friendship by helping communities develop agricultural, business, health, and education projects. Since the Peace Corps was founded in 1961, over 125,000 volunteers have gone through the program. More than 300 skills are needed, especially skills related to agriculture, industrial arts, engineering, and science. The host country determines which skills are needed where. Volunteers receive room, board, medical care, and transportation to the host country. At the end of their service, they receive a stipend for each month they worked. Only one applicant out of six is chosen for training, which lasts about three months. Volunteers normally serve for two years, but may serve longer. Information on volunteering can be obtained by dialing this toll-free number: (800) 424-8580 ext. 225.

The volunteers are supported by a small staff of regular employees. Information on these jobs is available from the Peace Corps, Office of Personnel, 1990 K St., NW, Washington, D.C. 20526.

RAILROAD RETIREMENT BOARD

In 1935, a law was passed that set up something like a social security program just for railroad workers. That system is still in existence. It is administered by the *Railroad Retirement Board,* which has 1,600 employees in 100 offices across the country. The Board hires computer specialists, contact representatives, and social insurance claims examiners, as well as the usual administrative and clerical workers. The headquarters is in Chicago. More information is available from the Director of Personnel, Railroad Retirement Board, 844 Rush St., Chicago, IL 60611; (312) 751-4580.

SECURITIES AND EXCHANGE COMMISSION

When the stock market crashed in 1929, many people thought something should be done to prevent the wild speculation that contributed to its collapse. The *Securities and Exchange Commission* was the result. It sets the rules for stockbrokers, mutual fund dealers, and other securities traders. Its staff of 1,900 includes experts in corporate law, financial analysis, accounting, and securities investigation. Additional employment information is available from the Director of Personnel, Securities and Exchange Commission, 450 Fifth St. NW., Washington, D.C. 20549; (202) 272-7067.

SMALL BUSINESS ADMINISTRATION

America's giant corporations started small. Fostering the creation and growth of the small business is the job of the *Small Business Administration*. In over 100 offices around the country, it employs about 4,500 specialists who can assist the small entrepreneur with finances, planning, legal matters, data processing, and administrative management. Major occupations in the Administration include loan specialist, law, and general business and industry specialist. Information about employment can be obtained from the Director of Personnel, Room 300, Small Business Administration, 1441 L St. NW., Washington, D.C. 20416; (202) 653-6567.

SMITHSONIAN INSTITUTION

"The nation's attic," as the *Smithsonian Institution* has been called, is a quasi-official agency that runs many different museums and a zoo. Employment totals about 5,000 in such occupations as guard, security officer, curator, and museum technician. Information for most of the Institution's components is provided by the Office of Personnel Administration, Smithsonian Institution, 900 Jefferson Drive, SW., Washington, D.C. 20560; (202) 357-1354.

STATE

The *Department of State* is responsible for conducting relations with foreign nations and international organizations. It has about 25,000 employees—about 35 percent in Washington and most of the rest in foreign countries. Career foreign service officers fill virtually all the professional positions in the 300-plus embassies and consulates around the world. *The Foreign Service is not under the Control of the Office of Personnel Management. It is administered directly by the Department.*

Appointments to the Foreign Service are made from among those who pass the *Foreign Service Officer Examination.* Candidates for these examinations must be at least 21 and under 57 years of age, unless they are either college graduates or juniors in college, in which case they can take the exam when they are 20. The test is generally given in December, the deadline for applications being in October. A booklet, ''Foreign Service Careers,'' and information about the exam, which is generally considered difficult, can be obtained from the Foreign Service Officer Recruitment Branch, Box 9317, Department of State, Rosslyn Station, Arlington, VA 22209.

Those who pass the exam and become foreign service officers usually serve in one of four specializations: administration, consular affairs, economic/commercial affairs, or politics. State is interested in people with training in political science, economics, public administration, and business administration. People with experience in business, government, and organizations involved in international activities are also sought.

Secretaries, foreign affairs analysts, general administrative and clerical workers, and passport and visa examiners are among the employees of the Department who are not members of the Foreign Service. Requests for information regarding opportunities and qualifications for these positions should be sent to the Recruitment Branch, Employment Division, U.S. Department of State, Washington, D.C. 20520; (202) 647-7152.

TENNESSEE VALLEY AUTHORITY

Controlling floods, developing forests, and producing electric power are among the activities of the Tennessee Valley Authority, a government-owned corporation with about 25,000 workers. Positions with the TVA are not covered by regular civil service procedures, so you must contact it directly. Guard, personnel management worker, miscellaneous administrator, engineering technician, general engineer, civil engineer, mechanical engineer, electrical engineer, facility management specialist, high voltage electrician, machinist, laborer, structural-ornamental ironworker, boilermaker, pipefitter, and carpenter are the occupations with the largest numbers of employees. Employment information is available at local facilities and construction projects and from the Employment Branch, Tennessee Valley Authority, 400 West Summit Hill Drive, Knoxville, TN 37902; (615) 632-7746.

TRANSPORTATION

The *Department of Transportation* implements the country's transportation policy through such agencies as the Federal Aviation Administration, Maritime Administration, Federal Railroad Administration, Urban Mass Transit Administration, National Highway Traffic Safety Administration, and Federal Highway Administration. The Coast Guard is also part of the Department during peace time.

The Department employs roughly 60,000 people. Air traffic controllers; electronics technicians; engineering technicians; general, civil, electrical, and electronics engineers; aviation safety officers; computer specialists; accountants, secretaries, and clerical workers hold most of the jobs. For employment information, it is best to contact the district or regional offices of the different agencies, inquiries concerning positions in Washington can be sent to the Central Employment Information Office, Office of Personnel and Training, U.S. Department of Transportation, Washington, D.C. 20590; (202) 366-9394. Applications are accepted only for announced vacancies.

The *Federal Aviation Administration* enforces safety regulations for airplanes and encourages the development of a national system of airports. Air traffic controllers and aeronautical engineers are among the many professional and clerical workers it employs. Further information is available about the Federal Aviation Administration, Employment Branch, APT-150, 800 Independence Ave. SW., Washington, D.C. 20591; (202) 267-8007.

The *Federal Highway Administration* administers the funding that makes it possible for states to build interstate highways. The FHA also regulates the activities of trucking companies that operate across state lines. It hires employees in a broad range of occupations, including civil engineering. For further information, write the Federal Highway Administration, Office of Personnel Training, HPT-22, 400 7th St. SW., Washington, D.C. 20590; (202) 366-0541.

The *Coast Guard,* sometimes called "The Navy of Mercy," *is the only branch of the Armed Forces not in the Defense Department.* Like the other armed services, it employs many civilians in a variety of occupations. The Coast Guard is primarily responsible for enforcing federal laws in American waters. Information about employment can be obtained from the Commandant (G-PC/ 62), U.S. Coast Guard, 2100 2nd St. SW, Washington, D.C. 20593; (202) 267-1706. Specify whether civilian or military employment interests you.

TREASURY

The *Department of the Treasury* is one of the original departments created by George Washington. With more than 155,000 employees, it is still one of the biggest departments. The following occupations each employ at least 1,000 people: computer specialist, criminal investigator, customs officer, financial institution examiner, internal revenue service agent, internal revenue service officer, lawyer, program analyst, tax accountant, and tax technician.

The Department has 11 major divisions: The Bureau of the Mint; Bureau of the Public Debt; Bureau of Alcohol, Tobacco, and Firearms; Bureau of Engraving and Printing; Bureau of Government Financial Operations; Federal Law Enforcement Training Center; Internal Revenue Service; Office of the Assistant Secretary for International Affairs; Office of the Comptroller of the Currency; U.S. Customs Service; U.S. Secret Service;

and U.S. Savings Bonds Division. The largest of these divisions are the Internal Revenue Service; U.S. Customs Service; Bureau of Alcohol, Tobacco, and Firearms; and Bureau of Engraving and Printing.

The *Internal Revenue Service* collects over 90 percent of the money owed the government by its citizens. It has about 4,500 employees in Washington and another 65,000 in the rest of the country. A substantial number of positions are filled by persons who majored in accounting, business administration, finance, economics, and law, but many other fields of study can also be applied to the work of the Service. There is an IRS office in or near your hometown to which you can write for additional employment information.

The *U.S. Customs Service* collects revenue from imports and enforces customs and related laws. It has 14,500 employees, about 1,400 of whom are located in Washington. The rest work at seaports, airports, border crossings, and other locations throughout the country. A small number are employed in foreign cities such as Montreal, Mexico City, London, Frankfurt, and Hong Kong. Among the workers it hires are customs patrol officers. Additional information about employment—including summer employment—is available from the Director, Personnel Management Division, Room 6124, U.S. Customs Service, 1301 Constitution Ave., Washington, D.C. 20229; (202) 634-5025.

The *Bureau of Alcohol, Tobacco, and Firearms* has two major functions: preventing the illegal production or sale of alcoholic beverages, tobacco products, and firearms; and regulating the legal producers of these products. Only about 500 of its 3,700 employees work in Washington; the rest are employed throughout the United States. For more information about employment, contact the Employment Branch, Bureau of Alcohol, Tobacco, and Firearms, 1200 Pennsylvania Ave. NW, Washington, D.C. 20226; (202) 566-7321.

The *Bureau of Engraving and Printing* has 3,000 employees, all of whom work in its Washington plant. They design, engrave, and print every American dollar bill, postage stamp, and food coupon. The Bureau employs printing and management specialists; chemists in ink, paper, and general research; mechanical, electrical, and industrial engineers; worker-trainees; apprentices in the mechanical trades; apprentices in the printing crafts; and many other workers. Employment information can be obtained from the Head, Personnel Staffing Branch,

Office of Industrial Relations, Bureau of Engraving and Printing, 14th and C Sts., Washington, D.C. 20228; (202) 447-9840.

DEPARTMENT OF VETERANS AFFAIRS

The *Department of Veterans Affairs* provides health care, financial aid, and other forms of assistance to America's veterans and their beneficiaries. It runs the largest health care system in the nation, with 172 hospitals, 218 outpatient clinics, 88 nursing homes, and 16 other facilities. The professionals employed in these institutions include physicians, dentists, pharmacists, nurses, physician assistants, psychologists, occupational therapists, physical therapists, social workers, medical technologists, dietitians, audiologists, and medical record librarians. Other major occupations are police officer, secretary, clerk-typist, biological technician, accounting technician, nursing assistant, diagnostic technician, radiological technician, medical machine technician, pharmacy technician, medical clerk, dental assistant, and supply clerk.

Besides providing medical care, the Department of Veterans Affairs administers such far-ranging benefit programs as compensation and pension funds for disabilities and death, home mortgage guarantees, job training, and educational assistance under the G.I. Bill.

Among the 200,000 white-collar employees of the Department of Veterans Affairs, besides those already mentioned, are veterans claims examiners, contact representatives, and the whole spectrum of clerical and administrative workers. In addition, there are about 45,000 blue-collar workers, mostly in food service and building maintenance occupations. Jobs for physicians, dentists, nurses, physician assistants, optometrists, and podiatrists are not under the jurisdiction of the Office of Personnel Management, but most of the other jobs are. For additional information, contact the personnel officer at any Department of Veterans Affairs facility.

THREE CITIES IN TEXAS

In the cities of Dallas, Houston, and Big Springs live many federal employees. The kind of work they do provides some idea of the variety of jobs available with the government in cities of different sizes all over the country.

The city of Dallas is one of the ten that serve as centers for the regional offices of most government agencies. (The others are Boston, New York, Philadelphia, Atlanta, Chicago, Kansas City, Denver, San Francisco, and Seattle.) Dallas has about 17,000 federal employees altogether. Since it is a regional headquarters, these employees work for almost every agency mentioned in this book. For example, the *Department of Health and Human Services* has approximately 1,600 employees in Dallas, who work in several of its major divisions, including the *Office of Education,* the *Food and Drug Administration,* and the *Social Security Administration.* The *Treasury Department* has more than 1,500 workers in Dallas, principally in the offices of the *Internal Revenue Service.* The offices of the other agencies, such as Agriculture, Commerce, and Transportation, are not as large; but taken together, all the jobs they offer add up to a substantial number.

The work done in the regional offices is a little like that done at the agency's headquarters and also a little like that done in any other field office. The administrators at the regional level do not formulate national policy, but they do ensure that national policies are enforced in their region. They serve as a link between the unwieldy national office and the numerous smaller field offices. The ordinary workers at the regional office do much processing and investigating.

Houston has thousands of federal workers; but, as is the case with Dallas and every other large city in America except Washington, the bulk of them work for the *Post Office.* The Houston Post Office employs more than 6,000 people. Another major employer, with more than 3,000 workers, is the *Veterans Administration.* Again, the situation is similar to that in Dallas; for even though there is a regional office of the Veterans Administration in Dallas, most of its employees do not work there. They work at the hospital, just as they do in Houston. In fact, Houston has more employees with the Veterans Administration than Dallas does.

Thousands of additional federal workers in Houston are employed at the *Johnson Space Center*. At first, you might think that this makes Houston different from other cities. After all, there is only one manned space flight center. But comparable installations do exist in most large cities—for example, the *Environmental Protection Agency* has a major research center near Raleigh, North Carolina, and the Census Bureau has a huge processing center in Jeffersonville, Indiana.

Many other agencies have employees working in Houston. The work these people do, it is worth repeating, is the *basic work of the government*. They are the people who see that a hungry family receives food stamps. They are the people who advise citizens about social security pensions. They are the people who help run a military base. Without them, the government would be merely a futile charade.

Big Springs shows what kinds of government jobs are found in hundreds of towns across the country. First, it is near an Armed Forces installation, Webb Air Force Base. Even without the Air Force, however, Big Springs would have hundreds of federal jobs. For example, the Department of Agriculture has field offices of the Research Service in Big Springs. These offices, and some others, give the Department a total of 27 employees in the town. Also, the Veterans Administration has a hospital in Big Springs that employs almost 400 people. There are another 50 or so federal employees at the Post Office. Obviously, too, where there is an airport, there are employees of the Federal Aviation Administration, four of them in this case. Put all these jobs together, and it turns out that Big Springs has about 1,200 federal employees—not as many as Washington, perhaps, but then the traffic isn't as bad.

AROUND THE WORLD

Despite the many positions available, opportunities for appointment to an overseas position are limited, because most federal jobs overseas are filled by local residents or by transfers who already work for the government. But among those government employees you do find working overseas, you will find almost every occupational field represented. There are construction and maintenance workers, doctors, nurses, teachers, technical experts, mining engineers, meteorologists, clerks, secretaries, typists, geologists, skilled craft workers, social workers, agricultural marketing specialists, and economists.

Agencies usually need only highly qualified and hard-to-find professionals, skilled technicians, and, in some cases, clerical and administrative personnel. A few agencies seek experienced teachers, librarians, nurses, and medical personnel. However, a few vacancies occur in most fields from time to time because of normal turnover and attrition.

Jobs are filled in United States territories, such as Guam and the Virgin Islands, by appointing local people who qualify in competitive examinations. Normally, the local labor market suffices for the needs of the government, and the positions are not publicized outside the local area. Sometimes, however, positions are filled by transferring career government employees from the United States.

In most foreign countries where the United States has installations, local people are also employed as much as possible. This is because it is almost always cheaper to employ local residents since no travel costs or overseas cost-of-living allowances need be paid.

There are certain general conditions that apply to most overseas appointments. Applicants usually must be at least 21 years old and in excellent physical condition, since employees may be required to live under difficult conditions and may not have complete medical facilities at hand. The minimum tour of duty is usually three years, but it is only one or two years in some areas. Employees in the middle grades and higher can usually bring their families with them, but agencies prefer single people for most clerical jobs. Appointments of both husband and wife to the same duty station are very uncommon, since the skills of both are rarely needed in the same place at the same time. If the duty station is fairly large, however, a spouse has a chance of finding employment, because, as previously mentioned, people already living in a country are usually given first shot at an opening. In addition to their regular pay, workers overseas frequently receive a post differential and either government housing or a housing allowance.

The largest employers of government personnel overseas are the Departments of State, Army, Navy, Air Force, Commerce, and Agriculture, the International Communications Agency, and the Peace Corps.

CHAPTER 8

THE U.S. POSTAL SERVICE

With 835,000 workers, the *U.S. Postal Service is the largest single employer of government workers other than the Defense Department.* It is also one of the fastest growing units of government. From 1980–1989, employment grew almost 25 percent. This, while many other agencies were losing workers due to budget constraints. Postal workers are the most widespread group of federal employees. There are 30,000 post offices and other postal facilities around the country, ranging in size from the corner of a rural grocery store to the blocks-long building in New York City, where over 40,000 workers keep the mail moving day and night. There are also 485 mail distribution centers. The range of jobs in the Postal Service is as great as the variety of buildings it owns or uses, but 90 percent of the white-collar workers are in just five occupations: postal clerk, mail carrier, mail handler, supervisor of the mails, and postmaster. Motor vehicle driver and maintenance workers are the largest blue-collar occupations.

POSTAL CLERKS

Postal clerks, who number about 380,000, include distribution clerks, distribution machine clerks, and window clerks.

Distribution clerks sort the mail—some by airmail or surface routes, others by ZIP code, city, or region; and others by delivery route. Some distribution clerks also keep records, cancel the stamps on mail that requires special handling, and work at the public windows in the post office.

Distribution machine clerks run the sorting equipment that helps reduce the need for distribution clerks. They first load the machines, making sure that all the envelopes face the same way. Then, as the machines present each letter to the operators, they read the ZIP Code and press a combination of keys to send the letter into its proper bin. The operator does this fifty times a minute, which requires sharp vision.

Window clerks are much more visible than the other clerks, who work behind the scenes. The window clerks sell stamps and money orders, give out mail, collect postage, listen to and act on complaints, answer questions, and explain the distinctions between first, second, third, and fourth class mail.

MAIL CARRIERS

The nation's 285,000 *mail carriers* are the last link of the chain that connects the letter writer to the letter reader. Carriers take the mail for their route and sort it in the sequence of delivery. They deliver the mail—by foot in cities, by car in rural areas—collect charges for postage and C.O.D. transactions, and pick up mail from people along their routes. Back at the post office, they readdress mail that has to be forwarded, make records of changes in addresses, and take care of other matters. One advantage of a mail carrier's job is being able to set one's own pace, so long as the last delivery is made on schedule. One disadvantage is summed up in the Postal Service motto: "Neither snow nor rain nor heat nor gloom of night stays these couriers from the swift completion of their appointed rounds."

Mail handlers are not nearly so numerous as carriers and clerks, though they still comprise a sizeable work force. Mail handlers load and unload trucks, trains, and planes, move bulk mail, operate canceling machines and forklifts, and repackage torn parcels.

Supervisors of the mails are administrators. They oversee the task of distributing and delivering the mail. They evaluate the work loads of carriers, make assignments, recommend changes in routes, see that the proper records are kept, and make sure that service at the public windows is as good as possible.

POSTMASTERS

Postmasters manage post offices. Their duties depend on the size of the post office of which they are in charge. Many postmasters work in very small post offices that are open for only a few hours a day. Such a post office might have window and general delivery operations and a rural delivery route—all supervised by the postmaster. In addition, the postmaster would be responsible for seeing that incoming mail was properly classified and that the proper records were kept. The postmaster's job in a city post office is much more complex. The postmaster needs many subordinates and would have to devote more time to personnel actions, planning, and management than the rural postmaster.

The Postal Service is the only agency of the federal government in which labor unions play an important part. Its hiring practices are also somewhat unusual. For the clerical and carrier positions, each post office and distribution center keeps its own list of eligible job seekers, although employment standards are set nationally.

Clerks and carriers must be at least 16 if they are high school graduates, and at least 18 if they are not. In actuality, relatively few people are hired before they are about 25, because of the length of the waiting periods before and after filing applications. Many postal workers transfer from other occupations. Applicants must pass a four-part written test and show that they can handle 70-pound mail sacks. They often start working part-time before advancing to a full-time position. Supervisors of the mails and postmasters are almost always chosen from the ranks of the clerks and carriers, since experience in the distribution and delivery of mail is a major qualification. *Postmasters are not political appointees.*

For more information about employment with the Postal Service, contact the personnel office of your local post office or the nearest mail distribution center. *They are the only places where you can find out when the employment tests are given and how to register for them.* Applications are accepted *only* when the post office decides that a test must be given; therefore, you might need to keep checking back before you actually file an application. The tests are given no more often than once every year or two and it may take as long as two years before someone who passed the test is hired. Some sample questions from one of the tests follow.

MAIL HANDLER EXAM

After applying to take a postal service exam, you will receive a sample test booklet. It will contain questions such as the examples which follow.

Sample Questions

1. Each of these five boxes contains four names. Match the forty names below the boxes with the letter at the top of each box. You have five minutes.

A	B	C	D	E
Redman	Denton	Teller	Edison	Wheeler
Payne	Rayburn	Moore	Miller	Forest
Carter	Sanford	Garvey	Appleton	Simmons
Conlow	Eastlake	Randall	Loman	Camp

1. Loman	11. Denton	21. Teller	31. Appleton
2. Edison	12. Payne	22. Simmons	32. Forest
3. Eastlake	13. Simmons	23. Payne	33. Moore
4. Garvey	14. Edison	24. Camp	34. Teller
5. Payne	15. Conlow	25. Miller	35. Carter
6. Miller	16. Randall	26. Garvey	36. Wheeler
7. Redman	17. Conlow	27. Randall	37. Edison
8. Carter	18. Randall	28. Wheeler	38. Rayburn
9. Denton	19. Eastlake	29. Redman	39. Loman
10. Sanford	20. Appleton	30. Moore	40. Sanford

2. How many of the following pairs of names are exactly the same?

(a) Misericordia Hospial	Miseracordia Hospital
(b) Lebonan Hospital	Lebanon Hospital
(c) Gouveneur Hospital	Gouverner Hospital
(d) German Polyclinic	German Policlinic
(e) French Hospital	French Hospital

The exam will contain many such sets of names, and you will be racing the clock, the whole exam lasting about two hours. In fact, most of the questions on the post office exams have time limits. Anyone who has enough time can find the correct answer; the problem is finding the correct answer *quickly*. General information is available from Headquarter Personnel Division, U.S. Postal Service, 475 L'Enfant Plaza, SW, Washington, D.C. 20260; (202) 268-3646.

CHAPTER 9

CONGRESS AND THE COURTS

Not all the jobs in the federal government are with the Executive branch, though the vast majority are. The Congressional and Judiciary branches of the government also employ thousands of workers in a large variety of jobs. These jobs and ways to learn about them are described in this chapter.

CONGRESS

Employees of the Congress—who number more than 38,000—include the staff members who work for a particular senator, representative, or committee, and the workers in three large agencies: The *General Accounting Office,* the *Government Printing Office,* and the *Library of Congress.*

Congressional staffers have some of the most interesting and most influential jobs in Washington—at least some staffers do; others just *think* they do. Still others thought they would, but learned otherwise when they started work and found that, like many glamorous jobs, working for a member of Congress often seems more exciting *before* you start to do it. New staffers are also sometimes disillusioned when they come face to face with the way Congress really operates. (Bills don't become laws in quite so neat a way as that described in civics textbooks.) And, strangely enough, others are disillusioned to learn that they have even more influence than they thought they would have, for these jobs really do bring you as close to the power centers of the government as you can get without winning an election.

ADMINISTRATIVE ASSISTANTS

The chief staff member is the *administrative assistant*. This person has usually worked closely with the senator or representative for many years. After the administrative assistant come the *legislative assistants,* who spend some time perfecting the language of bills to be introduced and somewhat more time answering the questions of constituents about the laws already passed or doing research for the member of Congress for whom they work. For example, if one of the committees on which the member sits is holding hearings on proposed legislation, the legislative assistant will research the subject of the legislation and prepare questions for the member to ask at the hearings. Some of the legislative assistants who do this sort of work are employed by the committee itself rather than a particular senator or representative.

CASE WORKERS

Case workers have less influence on new laws than do the legislative assistants, but they have more influence on the member's chances for re-election. Suppose, for example, that you disagree with a senator's stand on a new highway bill, but that the same senator helped your uncle straighten out a problem with his social security pension. That senator just might get your vote; and the case worker would be responsible. *Case workers deal with all the problems that constituents have with the government.* They make the phone calls and write the letters that prompt an agency to act to correct an error. They also send information about government programs to constituents.

CLERICAL WORKERS

In addition to the jobs unique to the Congress—administrative assistant, legislative aide, and case worker—every office also needs receptionists, typists, and secretaries. These jobs sometimes prove to be stepping-stones to other positions in Washington, either with the government or with private firms that deal extensively with the Congress.

Your state's senators and representatives can provide information about the availability of jobs in their offices. The positions often go to people who help the members in their elections.

DISADVANTAGES OF WORKING ON CAPITOL HILL

As already said, working on Capitol Hill can be exciting. It can also be nerve-wracking because all the jobs have one major drawback: Your boss could lose the next election. Another drawback is that although the Congress passes some of the most progressive labor laws in the world, it doesn't abide by them itself. Pay and fringe benefits are not uniform; there are no standard hiring practices; promotions are matters between the individual worker and the member, and staffers can be fired without notice. These drawbacks do not apply to jobs with the Congressional agencies, but then again, working for the agencies is not like working for Senator Longwind.

THE LEGISLATIVE BRANCH

The three largest agencies within the Legislative Branch are the *General Accounting Office, Government Printing Office,* and *Library of Congress.*

GENERAL ACCOUNTING OFFICE

The *General Accounting Office* is Congress's watchdog over the executive agencies. It reviews the particular programs of the agencies and also conducts government-wide reviews to ensure that programs are not duplicated in different agencies. To perform these reviews, its 5,000 plus employees—3,000 of whom are classified as GAO evaluators (GS399)—evaluate the cost, efficiency, and success of the programs. Naturally, the General Accounting Office employs many accountants and auditors. It also hires people with backgrounds in business, finance, economics, engineering, statistics, and computer science. In addition to performing audits, the office is responsible for settling claims against the government and collecting debts. A large staff of lawyers and claims examiners is employed for these purposes. More than half the agency's employees work in Washington. There are also more than 20 offices elsewhere in the United States. Further information is available from the Office of Personnel Management, Room 4452, General Accounting Office, 441 G St. NW., Washington, D.C. 20548; (202) 275-6092.

GOVERNMENT PRINTING OFFICE

The *Government Printing Office* is by turns a printer, a publisher, and a contract administrator. It actually prints about 10 percent of all government publications—most importantly, the *Federal Register* and the *Congressional Record*—and operates the largest printing plant in the world. What it cannot print itself, it has printed by commercial firms. It sells its publications through the mails and a chain of 26 bookstores. The Printing Office employs about 5,000 people, most of whom are blue-collar workers in the printing trades. The bulk of the employees work in Washington, but some are assigned to the regional bookstores and to 14 procurement offices located throughout the United States. Information on employment can be obtained from the Chief, Employment Branch, Government Printing Office, North Capitol and H Sts., NW, Washington, D.C. 20401; (202) 275-1137.

LIBRARY OF CONGRESS

In 1800, Congress appropriated $5,000 to buy some books. It now owns more than 15 million of them, including this one, and 45 million other items, ranging from movies to maps. These vast collections are housed in the *Library of Congress.* The Library's first responsibility is to conduct research and provide material to members of Congress, but it also administers the copyright law, maintains the *National Union Catalog,* distributes cataloging material for new publications, runs 159 regional and sub-regional libraries to serve the blind and physically handicapped, and provides reference services to the general public. The Library employs about 4,600 people; a large number of them have Master's degrees in library science, but other specialists are also hired. Almost all the jobs are located in Washington. Information about employment can be obtained from the Recruitment and Personnel Office, Library of Congress, 101 Independence Ave., SE, Washington, D.C. 20540; (202) 707-5000.

OTHER CONGRESSIONAL AGENCIES

Several smaller agencies are also part of the Congressional Branch. Their names, functions, and addresses follow:

Architect of the Capitol: maintains the buildings and grounds for Congress, the Library of Congress, and the Supreme Court; blue-collar employment exceeds 1,500; U.S. Capitol Building, Washington, D.C. 20515; (202) 225-1200.

United States Botanic Garden: collects and cultivates plants; 245 First St. SW., Washington, D.C. 20024; (202) 225-8333.

Office of Technology Assessment: identifies the consequences of the use of technology; 600 Pennsylvania Ave., SE, Washington, D.C. 20510; (202) 224-8713.

Congressional Budget Office: analyzes the cost of programs and estimates revenues; Second and D Streets SW., Washington, D.C. 20515; (202) 226-2621.

THE COURTS

The *Judicial Branch* of the federal government consists of the *Supreme Court* and a system of special and lower courts. Total employment of the courts is about 20,000. The jobs are very widely scattered around the country, however, each court doing its own hiring. The range of occupations is fairly small. Judges, law clerks, bailiffs, guards, and secretaries are among the people employed by the courts.

Federal cases start in the *district courts;* there is at least one in each state. There are more than 400 district judgeships in the United States. Next, a case goes to the *Courts of Appeals,* of which there are 97 divided among 11 circuits. Third and last comes the *Supreme Court.* There are also several special courts, such as the *Court of Claims,* the *Tax Court,* and the *Customs Court.*

Information about employment with a particular court can *only be provided by that court.* The addresses of the courts in any given city are listed in the *U.S. Government* section of local telephone books. Further information about the lower courts can be obtained from the Director, Administrative Office of the United States Courts, United States Supreme Court Building, Washington, D.C. 20544; (202) 633-6236.

CHAPTER 10

SUMMER JOBS, INTERNSHIPS, AND PART-TIME WORK

SUMMER JOBS

Next summer's job begins this fall if you want to work for the federal government. Each fall, usually in October or November, the Office of Personnel Management issues Announcement no. 414, ''Summer Jobs.'' It lists the openings agencies expect to have during the following summer and explains the application procedures. Most important, it gives the filing deadline, which varies from job to job, but may be as early as the second Friday in January and is rarely later than the middle of April. *Applications postmarked later than the deadline are not accepted.*

The first step in applying for a summer job is to call or write the nearest *Federal Job Information Center* and request that *Announcement 414* be sent to you. The second step is to learn what agencies have offices near you and call the personnel offices of these agencies. Ask when applications will be accepted for summer employment. If no decision has been made by the time you call, ask when you should call back. If the local offices have no information, write to the regional offices. Their addresses are provided in Announcement 414.

Summer jobs offer many of the same benefits as regular jobs. The pay is the same as that received by year-round workers in the same grade and, unlike the summer employees in private industry, summer workers in government earn vacation and sick leave. The months spent as a summer worker also count toward your total years of service if you later take a permanent job with the government.

Just as summer employees receive the same pay as their year-round counterparts, so must they meet the same general qualifications. This means that very few of the positions, even in the clerical group, are available for high school students. Except for a few trainee positions and jobs in the special programs described under Group V below, you must be at least 18 or a high school graduate to qualify for these jobs. Additional education or experience qualifies you for a higher grade.

SUMMER JOB CLASSIFICATIONS

The Office of Personnel Management classifies the various summer jobs available into five groups. Application procedures differ somewhat for each group; but, generally, you fill out an SF 171 form (see chapter 3, "A Form To Fill Out") and send a copy to each of the agencies for which you want to work. You must also send *OPM Form 1170/17,* which is a list of college courses and certificate of scholastic achievement.

Group I includes clerical occupations, such as statistical clerk or office machine operator, but the overwhelming majority of these jobs are for typists.

No written test is given for these jobs. At GS-1, the lowest level, no education or experience is required either, though you must be at least 18 if you are not a high school graduate. For GS-2, high school graduation or six months of experience is required; for GS-3, 1 year of college or experience; and for GS-4, two years of college or experience. The usual typing speed required is *40 words per minute,* verified when you get a job.

Group II jobs are for aides and technicians. They are far fewer than the clerical positions in Group I. Here is a list of the occupations included:

Accounting technician
Biological aide/technician
Computer operator
Economic assistant

Engineering aide/technician
Engineering draftsman
Firefighter
Guide
Health aide/technician
Illustrator
Lifeguard
Mathematics aide/technician
Medical aide/technician
Museum aide/technician
Nursing aide/technician
Park aide/technician
Physical science aide/technician
Recreation aide/technician
Surveying aide/technician

The education or experience you describe on the SF-171 must be related to the work you want to do.

Group III includes jobs for graduate students, law students, and college faculty members. The positions are far fewer in number than the people who want them. College placement offices have information on application procedures.

Group IV includes jobs for laborers and trades workers, such as animal caretakers and printing plant workers. No particular education or experience is normally required, but you must give evidence of your ability to do the work.

Group V jobs are for educationally and economically disadvantaged young people. These jobs are filled through the *Job Service,* which is listed in the *state government section of local telephone books.* To apply for these jobs, you must register with the Job Service and meet certain family income criteria. If no Job Service office serves your area, or if your Job Service office says it does not make referrals for these jobs, contact the *Office of Personnel Management's Federal Job Information Center nearest you.* Their addresses and phone numbers appear in Chapter 14, ''Help!''

GOVERNMENT INTERNSHIPS

A small number of government internships are available to outstanding college and graduate students. About two-thirds of the positions are located in Washington. The positions involve professional, administrative, or technical work of the kind usually done by college graduates. Grades range from GS-4 to GS-11, depending on the qualifications of the individual intern. Internships are often reserved for those returning to school in the fall.

The application procedure for internships differs from that for all other federal jobs. To begin with, you must be enrolled in a college or university that has been invited to nominate candidates for federal internships. These schools select candidates they feel will qualify for the internships specified by the various agencies. The agency offering the internship then chooses one candidate from all nominees. Needless to say, the competition is stiff. Moreover, being nominated is no guarantee of obtaining a position.

The specific requirements for a position depend on the nature of the work, but there are three general requirements:

1. Nominees must be graduate students, or undergraduates who will have sixty semester hours or ninety quarter hours by June of that year.
2. Graduate students must be in the *top half* of their class; undergraduates must be in the *top third*.
3. Nominees must demonstrate above-average leadership qualities in school and extracurricular activities.

If you are interested in an internship, *you should contact your school's placement office in January.* Internships are offered in most states. To obtain the most current listings, consult *A Directory of Public Service Internships,* published by the National Center for Public Service Internship Programs.

PART-TIME WORK

Part-time workers were becoming more common under President Carter; now they are becoming less common. Part-time workers earn money, sick leave, and vacations at the same rate as full-time employees. The experience gained can be useful in itself; in addition, once you are inside the system, you greatly increase your chances of being hired for a full-time position. If you do accept a part-time job, however, be sure you know whether it is permanent, so that you can keep it as long as you want it, or only temporary. Also, find out if you can be promoted.

Qualifications and application procedures for part-time positions are the same as those for full-time ones.

CHAPTER 11

SALARY AND OTHER BENEFITS

The salary of government workers compares favorably with that offered by private companies, especially at the lower grades. Other benefits enjoyed by federal job holders include paid vacations and sick leave, life and health insurance plans, training opportunities, transfer privileges between agencies, considerable job security, and retirement pensions.

SALARY

Step Increases

Several different salary schedules are used by the government. Thev can be divided among *General Schedule (GS), Wage Board Schedule (WG), Postal Service,* and all others. Since government salaries are adjusted annually to keep them aligned with the salaries of workers in the private sector, salary data are subject to change. In 1989, however, the starting salary for clerk-typists (GS-2) was $11,897, and for college graduates (GS-5), $16,305. Up-to date salary information is available from any government personnel office.

The GS pay system is used for most professional, administrative, clerical, technical, and scientific workers. About 45 percent of all federal employees are paid under the system.

In the GS system, you can receive two kinds of raises: step increases within the same grade and promotions from one grade to another. The first three step increases are scheduled at one-year intervals; the next three at 2-year intervals; and the last four at 3 year intervals. People are usually hired at the first step of a grade.

THE CAREER LADDER

Promotions to higher grades carry much larger raises than do the step increases. For most occupations, promotions are arranged in a career ladder. New employees are hired on the first or second rung of the ladder and promoted if they perform their jobs satisfactorily. The first two promotions may come only one year apart. Thereafter, the wait is longer, varying from employee to employee. Once employees reach the top rung of the career ladder for their position, they cannot be promoted—though they do receive step increases—unless they find a new position.

For clerical positions, most career ladders start at GS-1; high school graduates are hired at GS-2, however, so that is where most people start. The rungs of the ladder are one grade apart, and very few clerical positions have ladders reaching higher than GS-6, although some positions have ladders all the way up to GS-11.

For professional occupations, the bottom grade is often GS-5; the rungs are two grades apart, and promotions are rare after GS-12.

The *Wage Board Schedule (WG)* governs the pay of most blue-collar workers. The pay rate varies from place to place, so that government blue-collar workers are paid about the same amount as workers for private companies in the same area.

POSTAL SERVICE EMPLOYEES

Postal Service employees are paid according to yet another system. In fact, they are paid under several different schedules, depending on their occupations. For example, there are separate pay schedules for city mail carriers and rural ones. Employees receive periodic raises, which, because the workers are unionized, and the unions—unlike most unions in the government—are strong, tend to keep salaries relatively high. You can learn current pay rates for specific occupations *from any local post office.*

Finally, there are special salary plans for some agencies and employees. The Tennessee Valley Authority, the Federal Reserve Board, the

Foreign Service section of the State Department, and doctors and nurses employed by the Department of Veterans Affairs all have different salary systems.

PAID VACATIONS AND SICK LEAVE

Government employees earn annual leave, at rates based on the number of years they have been in government service. For the first three years, they earn four hours of leave every two weeks (13 vacation days a year); from their fourth to fifteenth years, six hours every two weeks (rounded to 20 days a year); and after 15 years, they earn eight hours every two weeks (26 days a year).

All full-time employees earn sick leave at the same rate: four hours every two weeks, or 13 days a year. Unused sick leave accumulates from year to year, making it an excellent form of insurance against lost income during long illnesses. Accumulated sick leave can also be credited toward retirement benefits.

LIFE AND HEALTH INSURANCE

Federal employees are offered several levels of Group Life Insurance for themselves plus optional coverage for their spouses and children. The government contributes to part of the cost of the premium for basic insurance, and the employee pays the balance through payroll deductions.

Many different health plans are available: Some are offered nation-wide; some are restricted to certain parts of the country, and some are reserved for employees of a particular union or association. New employees are given booklets describing the benefits offered under each plan they are eligible to join. Whenever the cost of the plans rises (which is just about every year), people can change plans.

TRAINING

Most large companies now give their employees vacations and health plans similar to those offered government employees. But few companies can match the range of opportunities for training found in the government. Training of some sort is provided for most new government employees. For some workers, such as FBI special agents and air traffic controllers, the training takes many weeks. For an apprentice in the blue-collar trades, it takes years. For most workers, however, training takes only a short period and may be of an informal nature.

ADDITIONAL (OPTIONAL) TRAINING

Employees can choose to attend special training programs during work. Clerical employees, for example, can attend classes in typing, English, or statistics. Employees at higher levels are offered seminars in managerial techniques, budgeting, and public speaking, among other subjects.

Employees can also attend college and graduate school classes at the government's expense—either during work hours or at other times—if they can show that the courses will help them improve their performance on the job. The amount of training employees can take at any time depends on the funds available, but all employees can take some training fairly regularly. Of course, all this training will do you little good if you still have the same job after you complete your training. That is where the next benefit comes in.

TRANSFER PRIVILEGES

Once you are hired, the sheer size of the federal government isn't likely to make much difference to you. You will work with a small group of people, just as you would with any company. But if you tire of your job, the size and scope of the government's employment opportunities will once more become important. As a federal employee, you will enjoy distinct advantages over people who don't work for the government when you transfer from job to job. You are a preferred candidate for many jobs, because the procedures another agency must follow to hire government workers are a little simpler than the ones followed to hire outsiders. Your accumulated leave, pension rights, and health insurance benefits are also transferable, something rarely allowed when you change jobs in the private sector.

JOB SECURITY

Incompetent government workers do get fired, and unneeded workers do get laid off. But they are not fired at the whim of a supervisor or laid off because of a short-term reduction in their work load. Before people can be fired, they must be given a written explanation of *why* they should be fired and allowed time to respond to the charges against them. If a decision is made to fire them, they can appeal to the head of their agency, the *Merit Systems Protection Board,* and, ultimately, *the courts.*

Layoffs are called "reductions in force." They occur when an agency's budget is slashed, when projects are completed, or when reorganizations make certain jobs unnecessary. Large-scale reductions in force are rare. More common are reductions that affect only a few people. Agencies do, however, make an effort to find new jobs for people laid off.

RETIREMENT

The government offers a retirement program called the Federal Employees Retirement System (FERS). FERS provides workers with benefits from three sources: a Basic Benefit Plan, Social Security, and a Thrift Saving Plan. Each pay period, the government and the employee make contributions to the Basic Benefit and Social Security portions of the plan. The government puts a contribution equal to one percent of the employee's pay each pay period through the Thrift Savings Plan account, which is automatically set up when the worker is hired. One of the strongest aspects of this retirement program is that many of the features are portable so that employees are still eligible for many of the benefits even if they leave federal employment.

CHAPTER 12

THREE GOVERNMENT WORKERS— WHY SOME PEOPLE WORK FOR THE GOVERNMENT

But why should you want to work for the government on any level? If you want to be a secretary, why should you handle correspondence for the Department of Veterans Affairs? If you want to be an engineer, why should you design dams for the Department of the Interior? If you want to be an artist, why should you illustrate pamphlets for the Department of Agriculture?

You will never know what a government career is like unless you have one, but you might get some idea from looking at the work done by three people. They are real people who actually made the decisions attributed to them. None of them has the kind of job often associated with the government. None is an astronaut, FBI agent, or politician. Their jobs are more typical than that.

The first, Martin Winston, will give you some idea of how people put together their own government careers; the second, Anna Hill, shows how people can benefit from government training programs; and the third, David Welsh, has a job that only the government can offer.

A FULL CAREER

Martin Winston strode out of his house under a sky as gray as the cement sidewalk he walked on. But Martin had spent enough time on airplanes to know that beyond the clouds, the sky was clear blue.

Martin's mood was as bright and clear as the sky above the clouds, for today he was going to retire. He couldn't help but think back over his career, a career during which he served five agencies of the American government and one agency of the United Nations. Not all the days had been as pleasant as this one promised to be—especially when he first looked for a job.

Martin graduated from college during the Depression. Back then, jobs were as hard to get as strawberries in January. He met many people like himself: people who were well trained, but still couldn't find work. He resolved to do what he could, so that people—especially young people—would be better prepared to make informed choices about careers. This would require that they know which educational and training programs to pursue, so that when the programs were completed, the graduates would have a fair chance of employment. But first, he needed a job for himself. He took a test, something like the college entrance exams today's high school students take. Martin's test didn't lead to college, though. It led to a job as a clerk.

Martin passed the test and worked as a clerk for several years. He became familiar with the first computers, studied for his Master's degree, and kept on the lookout for a better job. One day, he heard that the War Manpower Commission was revising the *Dictionary of Occupational Titles,* a basic tool for career counselors both then and now. Martin knew that by improving the *Dictionary,* he would improve the career counseling received by high school and college students. He applied for a job as an occupational analyst in the division that prepared the *Dictionary.* He got the job.

As an occupational analyst, Martin visited factories and other places of business and watched the workers. He saw what tasks they performed, learned the names of their jobs, and asked about the job titles of other employees with whom they worked. Back at the office, he wrote descriptions of the jobs he had studied.

Martin moved up while an analyst and was soon responsible for a complete section of the *Dictionary.* His division was moved to the Department of Labor, and things progressed smoothly until the early 1950s. At that time, the federal government laid off thousands of employees, including Martin.

His next position was with the Bureau of Labor Statistics. The new job had nothing to do with the analysis of occupations, and meant moving to New York, but it was better than unemployment. Martin did his work, which involved the collection of information about employment and earnings, bided his time, and waited for something better to turn up. After his division moved back to Washington, Martin heard that the *Dictionary* was hiring again. He returned to occupational analysis.

About this time, the International Labor Office, a specialized agency of the United Nations, decided that an *International Standard Classification of Occupations* was needed, so that people from different countries would have a common reference when they talked about jobs. Martin was the representative from the United States. He went to Geneva, Switzerland, where, with representatives from six other countries, he contributed to the new book.

During the year Martin spent in Geneva, he learned of many different ways to organize occupational material and became friends with experts on occupational analysis from all over the world. He was especially friendly with the Canadian representatives to various committees, who would soon incorporate the new methods into the Canadian occupational guide. In the 1970s, when the fourth edition of the *Dictionary* was prepared, Martin would use some of the ideas himself. But before the fourth came the third; and, after his stint with the UN, Martin returned to the United States to work on it.

While working again in the Division of Occupational Analysis, Martin heard about a new program in the Office of Education's Bureau of Vocational Training and Adult Education. Vocational training helps students most when it is closely related to particular occupations, and when students can get jobs related to their training. Martin worked to improve the coordination of training with specific occupations. He was doing what he wanted most to do and knew most about. During the time he spent with the Office of Education, he supervised the preparation of *Vocational Education and Occupations,* a book that can be used to organize data and guide students and counselors.

Martin next returned to the Bureau of Labor Statistics. While with the Bureau, he worked closely with the Office of Management and the Budget, which operates under the White House. The Office was developing a *Standard Occupational Classification Manual* to deal with a frequent problem in government, making sure that everyone is talking the same language. The government needs information in order to manage the economy. When the information is gathered, everybody must use the same set of definitions. Books like the *Manual* provide those definitions. Preparing such books might not be as glamorous as writing new laws, but it is important if the laws are to make any sense.

After helping with the *Manual,* Martin went back to work on the *Dictionary of Occupational Titles.* Now, he had the knowledge and experience needed to make real changes in it. The fourth edition was being prepared, and he incorporated many improvements that he had thought of while with the United Nations, the Office of Education, and the Bureau of Labor Statistics.

When Martin left his house on his way to his retirement luncheon, the fourth edition of the *Dictionary* had just been published. He thought his job was done. But a few days later, Martin heard from an old friend, a member of a special committee that had been formed to coordinate the work of all the government agencies that gather and distribute information about occupations. His friend wanted Martin to join in the task. Martin thought it over, took a deep breath, and agreed.

Martin went to work on a new book, something like the one he had done for the Office of Education. It would consolidate the information now found in many different volumes. Indeed, the book would bring together material from several stages of Martin's own career.

Since the above paragraph was written, the new book has been finished. Called *Vocational Preparation and Occupations,* it serves as a fitting capstone to the work of a dedicated public servant who accomplished what he set out to do: improve the public knowledge of occupations so that young people can receive better guidance when choosing a career.

TRAINING PAYS OFF

Anna Hill's face shines with the contented, confident expression of a woman who knows that she beat the odds. She has worked her way up from secretary to editor on one of the most distinguished journals published by the government, the *Monthly Labor Review.* Her climb wasn't easy, and the path she took is not well marked. But today she can look back on her achievement and say, "That was well done."

Anna worked as a receptionist for a lawyer and a doctor when she first came to Washington. The job was varied and provided good experience. After a while, Anna moved on to a clerical job with the government. Uncle Sam didn't pay as much as the lawyer and doctor had, but the government offered much better opportunities for advancement, which Anna made the most of.

Anna was working as a secretary when her agency announced a new training program that prepared participants for positions as economists. The agency stressed that the training would take a long time and that new jobs were not guaranteed. Still, Anna signed up, seeing it as her chance to get the college-level training she wanted.

At the end of the training period, Anna's supervisor helped her get placed in her current position. Anna says she was lucky. Her supervisor supported her, and she worked for an agency that offered just the kind of training she could use. Perhaps she *was* lucky, at least in part. To benefit from government training, you often do need to be in the right place at the right time. But others might say that Anna made her own luck. After all, her supervisor couldn't have helped her had she not shown interest and promise, and the training would have been wasted had she not had the ability to apply it.

Anna's current job as an editor makes full use of the training she received. She evaluates articles on labor economics that have been written by some of the most notable people in the field. She must be constantly alert to the originality of an author's theory and the validity of the statements made. Anna recommends that an article be accepted for publication or rejected. Once accepted, the article still needs to be edited. Anna determines what the author's main points are and makes sure that they are clear to the reader and supported by the article. Sections of the article may need minor revisions or major rewriting. When satisfied that the article is ready for publication, Anna confers with the author to ensure that the changes she has made are acceptable. That ends the most challenging part of her job. But before the public reads the article, Anna will read it several more times at various stages, from manuscript to magazine, to see that no errors appear in the finished product. Within two months, the article will be on the desks of the magazine's readers. By that time, Anna will have turned her attention to new articles.

ONLY IN GOVERNMENT

Poisons eating away at a worker's lungs would be one of the last things you would think of if you met David Welsh. Young, handsome, his face ringed by a soft, brown beard, he radiates the energy of a corporate lawyer on the rise. He needs that energy to do his job, for his work is basic to the task of governing a modern society: he writes regulations. Some of his regulations restrict the use of poisons that cause lung disease. Others deal with the use of special equipment, the safety of the places people work, or the control of poisons, such as arsenic.

David is an industrial hygienist with the Occupational Safety and Health Administration, but he did not grow up wanting to be one. In fact, when he was growing up, industrial hygiene was almost unheard of and the Occupational Safety and Health Administration did not exist. Since then, our awareness of how we have poisoned our environment has grown, and the need for people like David has increased.

When the shortage of industrial hygienists first became evident, David was preparing for a career in medicine. But instead of going to medical school right after college, he decided to enter a graduate program in industrial hygiene. He liked it, and a year later felt that he could make as great a contribution to people's health by working as an industrial hygienist as he could as a doctor.

The cast iron dome of the nation's Capitol looms over the building in which David now works. This is only right, after all, for David's work is an extension of the lawmaking power of Congress. The major laws passed by Congress are not intended to cover particulars. They might be thought of as general statements of the will of the people, rather than as detailed lists of prohibited or required acts. To clarify how the general law applies in a particular situation, regulations must be written. That's where David comes in. The regulations he writes clarify the *Occupational Health and Safety Act*. According to the Act, workers have the right to a safe environment. David helps determine what a "safe environment'' is. Jobs like his, involving the preparation of legally binding regulations, are found only with the government.

There are almost as many stages to writing a regulation as there are movies about the Old West. First, officials decide what regulations—or standards, as they are called in the Occupational Health and Safety Administration—are needed. David doesn't just decide to write a regulation himself, although he does make recommendations. Once a decision is made, an industrial hygienist and a lawyer are given the task of preparing the standard.

Let's say David has to write a regulation on a dangerous substance widely used in industry and government. We'll call it basic solvent stuff, or BSS for short. He begins by gathering information, a job that continues until the regulation is signed. He'll consult with experts, search out scientific papers, and—along with the lawyers assigned to the case—consult with experts and conduct hearings until he knows as much about BSS as can be known. When he's ready, he'll write a draft of the regulation and publish it in the *Federal Register,* where all regulations are first printed, inviting comment from all interested parties—unions, industry representatives, consumer groups, Congress, other government agencies, and individual citizens. The process of writing drafts and inviting comments is repeated until there is some agreement on how the regulation should read and what it means. This can mean more than a year of hearings, revisions, and reviews. Finally, the standard is ready to be signed by the head of the Occupational Safety and Health Administration. Once signed, it has the same weight as the law passed by Congress that made the regulation necessary.

After a regulation is signed, the task of ensuring the safety of America's workers passes on to the inspectors employed by the agency. Meanwhile, David starts to research another dangerous substance.

The experiences of Martin Winston, Anna Hill, and David Welsh demonstrate why some people work for the government. Their careers gave them a chance to make a decent salary, advance in their profession, and contribute to the good of society. Perhaps the last reason is the most important, the one that outweighs some of the disadvantages of government work that are described in the next chapter.

CHAPTER 13

UNREACHABLE GOALS AND OTHER DRAWBACKS OF GOVERNMENT JOBS

Government employment offers some very great rewards: No other employer can match the variety of jobs to be done nor the complexity of the problems to be solved. Government employment also has some serious drawbacks. The extent of these drawbacks will largely depend on how satisfying your particular job is. If it is challenging and rewarding, the drawbacks are not likely to concern you—at least not most of the time. If your job is not stimulating, however, government employment can make you feel like a man who overeats at a second-rate restaurant; he starts out disliking the food, but ends up hating himself for wolfing it down.

The drawbacks of government employment concern prestige, politicians, promotions, and the very problems that the government tries to solve. The last might be the most important.

TRYING TO SOLVE UNSOLVABLE PROBLEMS

The village blacksmith in Longfellow's poem begins a new task each day and completes it by quitting time. The government seems to begin jobs readily enough, but finishing them is something else again. Indeed, many of the government's tasks can never be finished. Jobs like defending the country and protecting the rights of all citizens demand unflagging zeal. Government workers must accept the fact that they try to solve unsolvable problems and try to reach a goal that always stays within sight, but out of reach. Sometimes the government does fix on an attainable goal. When it does, thousands of workers can take pride in helping make possible the giant leap that carried us to the moon. But more usually, there is no such grand climax. There is simply the ongoing task of maintaining the country. People who believe that they can come to Washington and change the world with a few months work are courting frustration and disillusionment.

More typical of government action than the moon shot is an antitrust suit brought against IBM when Lyndon Johnson was president. The case had not been settled ten years, six attorneys general, and three presidents later. Not a single person who began the case was still with it in 1979. Then the case was dropped. In ten years, no one had the blacksmith's satisfaction.

POLITICS AND PROMOTION: AN UNEASY MARRIAGE

The promotion system in the federal service is a mixed blessing. Promotions are almost automatic, at least at the start of a career, leaving little room for individual recognition. When everyone is treated as average, people stop trying to be superior and lose the satisfaction of believing themselves among the best. As a result, a job that began as a challenge becomes a bore. The situation is worst, according to many government workers, when a bored employee is promoted into a supervisory position. Such supervisors have built their careers on doing no more than the minimum. An employee who wants to push a program to the maximum soon finds such supervisors immovable barriers to achieving excellence.

Politics and the world of the career civil servant are unrelated to each other in civics textbooks and the promotional literature published by government agencies. In reality, the two have an uneasy marriage. Some agencies and some programs are relatively isolated from political concerns. Most are not. Every new president has his own priorities. Slowly but surely, these priorities are reflected in the federal budget. When they are, yesterday's Cinderella program becomes today's old grey mare. People don't usually get fired, but new ones don't get hired, either, and the program withers away from lack of interest and tired blood.

LACK OF PRESTIGE AND OTHER DRAWBACKS

Prestige cannot be held in your hand. It won't help put tacos on the table or T-shirts on your back. But it contributes a great deal to job satisfaction. The prestige of a job cannot be measured very easily, either; yet everyone seems to know that, socially, a doctor is a step above a lawyer, and lawyers outrank accountants. Everyone also seems to know that a doctor in private practice has more prestige than one who works for the government, that a lawyer with a private firm outranks one with the government, and that accountants with private corporations are better thought of than ones who work for the government.

Government jobs, except for those at the very top, are low in prestige. Tell people you work for the government, and they seem forced to say, "I guess you don't work too hard then. You government workers have it made." Usually remarks like that don't mean much, but they are so common that one is bound to hit you on a day when you started work early, skipped lunch, and had to put in some overtime, so that four different projects—all set up by people elected by the person making the remark, in order to serve the person making the remark—could move forward.

Some drawbacks are related to each other. Politicians have a history of appointing people to jobs because the job seeker helped the politician get elected, rather than because the job seeker is qualified. Therefore, the civil service was set up a hundred years ago to make sure that qualified people were hired by the government and that a newly elected politician could not fire all the workers of the opposite political party. One unfortunate result of the need to isolate the civil service from politics is that some marginal workers become entrenched in positions they are no longer fit to hold.

One other drawback of government jobs, despite the conventional wisdom, is that some don't pay well. The GS pay system is fairly rigid. It is the same throughout the country, and when cost-of-living adjustments are given—as they are most years—they are usually a flat percentage increase for all grades and steps. For these reasons, and because of the way occupations are grouped together, some government employees would be better paid by private firms. For example, writer-editors fresh out of college receive relatively high wages in government jobs, but experienced lawyers do not. And federal employees in the South are better paid in relation to their cost of living than employees in the North and Far West. Furthermore, no one who is honest becomes rich in a government job. Government workers do not command the exorbitant incomes of very successful doctors, lawyers, sales representatives, or executives. And even though most government salaries are fairly good, salaries are going down relative to the national average. Representatives, senators, and presidents find it difficult to give a full cost-of living increase to government workers. They find it easier to complain about the workers, lower their salaries, and then complain some more.

Fringe benefits, too, are sometimes not as good as those found in strongly unionized industries or major corporations. The government's reputation for good fringe benefits is largely based on what it did 50 years ago. Since then, other employers have matched or surpassed them. Two exceptionally good fringe benefits in the government are the policies on sick leave and annual leave, which are extremely generous. However, the government offers no stock options, employee discounts, or Christmas bonuses, all of which can add substantially to a worker's salary (some of the addition being sheltered from taxes). Also, health plans and life insurance policies offered to government workers are sometimes not as good as those available to workers with large, private companies.

None of these drawbacks is very important in itself, but taken together they can be formidable. You should think about them before you go looking for a government job. Like a small pebble in your shoe, they seem unimportant at first, but they can make you awfully sore.

CHAPTER 14

"HELP!"

You can get help in finding a government job by visiting the right places, reading the right material, and contacting the right people. This chapter tells you where to visit, what to read, and whom to contact.

VISIT

Two places to visit are the office of a *school counselor or placement service—even if you are not in school—*and the nearest *Job Service Office.* The counseling or placement office should have some of the reading material described in the next section of this chapter. Counselors should also know about the local job market and be able to give you the names of former students who now work for the government. The amount of help an office can provide to someone who does not or did not attend the school varies widely. As a minimum, however, you should be able to use some of the printed material. You will also be able to scan the bulletin boards for information about local job possibilities.

Job Service offices are run by your state's government. Their addresses are listed in the *state government* section of local phone books. The Job Service office should have the most up-to-date material available about government jobs. Counselors there can also give aptitude tests, suggest training programs, and assist you in finding a job.

BOOKS

Several kinds of books can help you if you are interested in a government career: books about the occupation you want to enter, books about the government, and books about job hunting. Books have been written about almost every occupation in which you could possibly be interested. Many are listed on the last page of this one. Your librarian can help you find others. In addition, there are some very large books that describe hundreds of occupations. Two are published by the government, but they are not restricted to government occupations. They are the *Dictionary of Occupational Titles* and the *Occupational Outlook Handbook*. Most people only want to read a few pages in these books, so, instead of buying them, look for them in a library.

Several books and pamphlets deal only with the government. Most are published by the government, and some are no more trustworthy than other recruiting literature. Some are free, some aren't. Before buying a government book or pamphlet, contact the agency that published it; you can often get a single copy free. Sometimes, members of Congress obtain free copies of government publications for their constituents.

Here are some useful books published by the government. The first two are *not* available free of charge.

U.S. Government Manual, published each year by the General Services Administration, Office of the Federal Register. It contains almost 900 pages of names, addresses, telephone numbers, and descriptions for every federal agency. Sources of information about employment are usually given.

Qualification Standards for White-Collar Positions Under the General Schedule is published by the Office of Personnel Management. It fills two fat looseleaf binders, and there is a companion volume for blue-collar work. They are supplemented by position descriptions for all the government occupations. The position descriptions are small booklets, but their number makes up for their size. Also, there are comparable looseleaf books for the qualification standards for occupations with the U.S. Postal Service. The descriptions of jobs in this book are distilled from all these volumes. These books are not readily available, and they are written in a language peculiar to personnel offices. However, it is this last feature which makes them worth searching out; their language is the language you want to use on your application form. The books—sometimes on microfiche—can be found in their true home: the personnel offices of government agencies. They're also at the *Federal Job Information Centers.* Incidentally, the fat book for white-collar jobs is always called X-118; the blue-collar manual is X-118A. Occupations are listed by their GS or WG number; these numbers are given along with the job titles throughout this book.

Among the timely books not published by the government is the *College Placement Annual.* It gives current information each year about government and nongovernment hiring plans. Published by the College Placement Council, it is available through college placement offices.

In addition to the *Federal Manual* described above, there are several commercially published directories to government offices. You can use them to find the names of more people to contact. Two of the most complete are the *Washington Information Directory* published by Congressional Quarterly and the *Federal Yellow Book* published by the Washington Monitor, Inc. The first is arranged by subject; the second is by agency. Telephone books are the easiest way to find agencies in nearby cities and towns; the library should have them.

Job-hunting manuals have proliferated in recent years. Two good ones are the following: *What Color Is Your Parachute?* by Richard N. Bolles (Berkeley, California: Ten Speed Press, 1991); and *Joyce Lain Kennedy's Career Book* by Joyce Lain Kennedy and Dr. Darryl Laramore (Lincolnwood, Illinois: NTC Publishing, 1988).

Besides books, magazines—especially those aimed at young people—often have articles on jobs and job hunting. Some magazines, such as *Career World* and the *Occupational Outlook Quarterly,* are devoted exclusively to these subjects.

FEDERAL JOB INFORMATION CENTERS

Current Federal job opportunities information is available by touch tone telephone. You may call the Federal Job Information Center, seven days a week, 24 hours a day for a variety of topics on Federal employment, including such subjects as jobs for which applications are being accepted, student programs, and summer employment. Of course, job announcements and the all important SF-171 are also available at Federal Job Information Centers.

Alabama

Huntsville:
Building 600, Suite 341
3322 Memorial Pkwy., South,
35801-5311

Alaska

Anchorage:
222 W. 7th Ave., #22
99513-7572

Arizona

Phoenix:
Century Plaza Bldg., Rm. 1415
3225 N. Central Ave., 85012

Arkansas

(See Oklahoma Listing)

California

Los Angeles:
9650 Flair Drive
Ste. 100A
El Monte, 91731

Sacramento:
4695 Watt Ave., North Entrance
95660-5592

San Diego:
Federal Bldg., Room 4-S-9
880 Front St., 92188

San Francisco:
P.O. Box 7405, 94120
(Located at 211 Main St., 2nd Floor,
Room 235)

Colorado

Denver:
P.O. Box 25167, 80225
(Located at 12345 W. Alameda
Pkwy., Lakewood)

Connecticut

Hartford:
Federal Bldg., Room 613
450 Main St., 06103

Delaware

(See Philadelphia Listing)

District of Columbia

Metro Area:
1900 E St., N. W., Room 1416
20415

Florida

Orlando:
Commodore Bldg., Suite 150
3444 McCrory PL, 32803-3701

Georgia

Atlanta:
Richard B. Russell Federal Bldg.,
Room 940A, 75 Spring St., S.W.,
30303

Hawaii

Honolulu (and other Hawaiian Islands
and Overseas):
Federal Bldg., Room 5316
300 Ala Moana Blvd., 96850

Idaho

(See Washington Listing)

Illinois

Chicago:
175 W. Jackson Blvd., Room 530
60604

Indiana

Indianapolis:
Minton-Capehart Federal Bldg.,
575 N. Pennsylvania St., 46204
(For Clark, Dearborn, & Floyd
Counties, see Ohio listing)

Iowa

(For Scott County see Illinois listing;
for Pottawatamie County, See Kansas
listing)

Kansas

Wichita:
One-Twenty Bldg., Room 101
120 S. Market St., 67202

Kentucky

(See Ohio listing; for Henderson
County, see Indiana listing)

Louisiana

New Orleans:
1515 Poydras St., Suite 608, 70112

Maine

(See New Hampshire Listing)

Maryland

Baltimore:
Garmatz Federal Building
101 W. Lombard Street, 21201

Massachusetts

Boston:
Thos. P. O'Neill, Jr. Federal Bldg.
10 Causeway St., 02222-1031

Michigan

Detroit:
477 Michigan Ave., Rm. 565, 48226

Minnesota

Twin Cities:
Federal Building, Room 501
Ft. Snelling, Twin Cities, 55111

Mississippi

(See Alabama Listing)

Missouri

Kansas City:
Federal Building, Rm. 134
601 E. 12th Street, 64106
(For Counties west of and including
Mercer, Grundy, Livingston, Carroll,
Saline, Pettis, Benton, Hickory,
Dallas, Webster, Douglas, and Ozark)

St. Louis:
400 Old Post Office Bldg.
815 Olive St., 63101
(For all other Missouri Counties not
listed under Kansas City above)

Montana

(See Colorado Listing)

Nebraska

(See Kansas Listing)

Nevada

(See Sacramento, CA Listing)

New Hampshire

Portsmouth:
Thomas J. McIntyre Federal Bldg.
Room 104
80 Daniel Street, 03801-3879

New Jersey

Newark:
Peter W. Rodino, Jr., Federal Bldg.
970 Broad Street, 07102

New Mexico

Albuquerque:
Federal Building
421 Gold Avenue, S.W., 87102

New York

New York City:
Jacob K. Javits Federal Bldg.
26 Federal Plaza, 10278

Syracuse:
James H. Hanley Federal Building
100 S. Clinton Street, 13260

North Carolina

Raleigh:
P. O. Box 25069
4505 Falls of the Neuse Rd.
Suite 450, 27611-5069

North Dakota

(See Minnesota Listing)

Ohio

Dayton:
Federal Building, Rm. 506
200 W. 2nd Street, 45402
(For Van Wert, Auglaize, Hardin,
Marion, Crawford, Richland,
Ashland, Wayne, Stark, Caroll,
Columbiana Counties and all
Counties north of these see Michigan
listing)

Oklahoma

Oklahoma City:
(Mail only)
200 N. W. Fifth St., 2nd Floor, 73102

Oregon

Portland:
Federal Bldg., Room 376
1220 S.W. Third Ave., 97204

Pennsylvania

Harrisburg:
Federal Bldg., Room 168
P.O. Box 761, 17108

Philadelphia:

Wm. J. Green, Jr., Federal Bldg.
600 Arch Street, 19106

Pittsburgh:

Federal Building
1000 Liberty Ave., Rm. 119, 15222

Puerto Rico

San Juan:
Frederico Degetau Federal Building
Carlos E. Chardon Street
Hato Rey, P.R. 00918

Rhode Island

Providence:
Pastore Federal Bldg.
Room 310, Kennedy Plaza
02903

South Carolina

(See Raleigh, NC listing)

South Dakota

(See Minnesota Listing)

Tennessee

Memphis:
200 Jefferson Avenue
Suite 1312, 38103-2335

Texas

Dallas:
(Mail or phone only)
1100 Commerce St., Rm. 6B12,
75242

San Antonio:
8610 Broadway, Rm. 305, 78217

Utah

(See Colorado Listing)

Vermont

(See New Hampshire Listing)

Virginia

Norfolk:
Federal Building, Room 500
200 Granby St., 23510-1886

Washington

Seattle:
Federal Building
915 Second Ave., 98174

West Virginia

Phone only:

Wyoming

(See Colorado Listing)

ADDITIONAL READING

College Placement Annual. Bethlehem, Pennsylvania: College Placement Council, annual.

Federal Yellow Book. Washington: Washington Monitor, Inc., annual.

Krannich, Ronald L. and Caryl Rae Krannich. *Find a Federal Job Fast! Cutting the Red Tape of Getting Hired.* Woodbridge, Virginia: Impact Publications, 1990.

Lott, Catherine S. and Oscar C. Lott. *How to Land a Better Job.* Lincolnwood, Illinois: NTC Publishing Group, 1989.

U.S. Department of Labor. Bureau of Labor Statistics. *Occupational Outlook Quarterly.*

U.S. Department of Labor. Bureau of Labor Statistics. *Occupational Outlook Handbook.* Washington: Government Printing Office, revised every two years.

U.S. General Services Administration. Office of the Federal Register. *U.S. Government Manual.* Washington: Government Printing Office, annual.

U.S. Office of Personnel Management. "Current Federal Examination Announcements." Washington: Office of Personnel Management, irregular.

Waelde, David E. *How To Get A Federal Job,* 5th edition. Washington, D.C.: FEDHELP Publications, 1989.

Washington Information Directory. Washington: Congressional quarterly, annual.

INDEX OF COLLEGE MAJORS AND FEDERAL JOBS

This index can be used like a road map. It will help you locate federal agencies and departments that are seeking individuals with your academic major, related field of study or experience for their typical entry-level position.

Under each academic major, you will find the names of the agencies and departments interested in individuals with that background. If an agency is a component of a department or larger agency, you will find the parent organization's name in parentheses and bold faced. Independent agencies stand without parenthetical reference.

This list is reprinted from the *Federal Career Directory,* published by the Office of Personnel Management, 1990.

Accounting

Administrative Office of the U.S. Courts
Agency for International Development
Agricultural Stabilization and
  Conservation Service (**Agriculture**)
Agriculture, Department of
Army Corps of Engineers (**Defense**)
Army Finance and Accounting Center
  (**Defense**)
Army Materiel Command (**Defense**)
Army Military District of Washington
  (**Defense**)
Bureau of Economic Analysis
  (**Commerce**)

Bureau of Engraving and Printing
  (**Treasury**)
Bureau of Prisons (**Justice**)
Bureau of the Public Debt (**Treasury**)
Commodity Futures Trading Commission
Defense Contract Audit Agency (**Defense**)
Defense Logistics Agency (**Defense**)
Departmental Offices (**Treasury**)
Drug Enforcement Administration (**Justice**)
Energy, Department of
Equal Employment Opportunity
  Commission
Export-Import Bank of the United States
Executive Office of the President

ACTUARIAL SCIENCE

ADP

ADULT EDUCATION AND TRAINING

ADVERTISING

AERONAUTICAL ENGINEERING

AEROSPACE ENGINEERING

AGRIBUSINESS MANAGEMENT

AGRICULTURAL BUSINESS

AGRICULTURAL ECONOMICS
Agricultural Stabilization and
  Conservation Service **(Agriculture)**
Economics Management Staff
  (Agriculture)
Farm Credit Administration **(Agriculture)**
International Trade Commission

AGRICULTURAL ENGINEERING
Agricultural Research Service
  (Agriculture)

AGRICULTURAL FINANCE
Farm Credit Administration **(Agriculture)**

**AGRICULTURAL
MANAGEMENT**
Agricultural Marketing Service
  (Agriculture)
Agricultural Stabilization and
  Conservation Service **(Agriculture)**

AGRICULTURE (GENERAL)
Agricultural Marketing Service
  (Agriculture)
Agricultural Stabilization and
  Conservation Service **(Agriculture)**

AGRONOMY
Agricultural Research Service
  (Agriculture)

AIRWAY SCIENCE
Federal Aviation Administration
  (Transportation)

ALL MAJORS
ACTION
Air Force **(Defense)**
Army Information Systems Command
  (Defense)
Army Materiel Command **(Defense)**
Training and Doctrine Command **(Defense)**
Bureau of Alcohol, Tobacco, and Firearms
  (Treasury)
Bureau of Labor Statistics **(Labor)**

Defense Investigative Service **(Defense)**
Employment and Training Administration
  (Labor)
Employment Standards Administration
  (Labor)
Equal Employment Opportunity
  Commission
Federal Aviation Administration
  (Transportation)
Federal Deposit Insurance Corporation
Federal Highway Administration
  (Transportation)
General Services Administration
Immigration and Naturalization Service
  (Justice)
Labor, Department of
Maritime Administration **(Transportation)**
Military Traffic Management Command
  (Defense)
Mine Safety and Health Administration
  (Labor)
National Science Foundation
Occupational Safety and Health
  Administration **(Labor)**
Office of Inspector General **(Labor)**
Office of Personnel Management
Office of the Secretary **(Health and
  Human Services)**
Railroad Retirement Board
State, Department of
U.S. Marshals Service **(Justice)**
U.S. Postal Service
Veterans Affairs, Department of

AMERICAN HISTORY
National Archives and Records
  Administration

AMERICAN STUDIES
National Archives and Records
  Administration

**ANIMAL HEALTH
TECHNOLOGY**
Animal and Plant Health Inspection
  Service **(Agriculture)**

ANIMAL HUSBANDRY
Agricultural Marketing Service
(Agriculture)

ANIMAL SCIENCE
Agricultural Marketing Service
(Agriculture)
Bureau of Land Management **(Interior)**

ANTHROPOLOGY
Bureau of Land Management **(Interior)**
U.S. Customs Service **(Treasury)**

ARCHAEOLOGY
Bureau of Land Management **(Interior)**
Forest Service **(Agriculture)**
National Endowment for the Humanities,
National Park Service **(Interior)**

**ARCHITECTURAL
ENGINEERING**
Navy **(Defense)**
U.S. Postal Service

ARCHITECTURE
Army Corps of Engineers **(Defense)**
Farmers Home Administration
(Agriculture)
General Services Administration
Housing and Urban Development,
Department of
National Institute of Standards and
Technology **(Commerce)**
Navy **(Defense)**
Veterans Affairs, Department of

AREA STUDIES
U.S. Information Agency
Voice of America **(U.S. Information
Agency)**

ART (DESIGN)
Government Printing Office

ART HISTORY
National Archives and Records
Administration
Smithsonian Institution

ASIAN LANGUAGES
National Security Agency

**ASTRONAUTICAL
ENGINEERING**
National Aeronautics and Space
Administration

ASTRONAUTICS
National Aeronautics and Space
Administration

ASTRONOMY
Defense Mapping Agency **(Defense)**
Navy **(Defense)**

AUDIOLOGY
Veterans Affairs, Department of

AUDITING
Departmental Offices **(Treasury)**
Housing and Urban Development,
Department of
National Credit Union Administration
Office of Inspector General **(Commerce)**
(Labor)
State, Department of

BANK LAW
Office of the Comptroller of the Currency
(Treasury)

BANKING
Farm Credit Administration **(Agriculture)**
Office of the Comptroller of the Currency
(Treasury)
Small Business Administration
State, Department of

BIOLOGICAL LAB TECHNOLOGY

Animal and Plant Health Inspection
Service **(Agriculture)**

BIOLOGICAL SCIENCES

Environmental Protection Agency
Library of Congress

BIOLOGY

Animal and Plant Health Inspection
Service **(Agriculture)**
Army Corps of Engineers **(Defense)**
Bureau of Indian Affairs **(Interior)**
Bureau of Land Management **(Interior)**
Bureau of Reclamation **(Interior)**
Federal Bureau of Investigation **(Justice)**
Forest Service **(Agriculture)**
Minerals Management Service **(Interior)**
Navy **(Defense)**
Office of Surface Mining Reclamation and
Enforcement **(Interior)**
Patent and Trademark Office **(Commerce)**
U.S. Fish and Wildlife Service **(Interior)**

BOTANY

Bureau of Land Management **(Interior)**

BROADCASTING

U.S. Information Agency

BUDGET ANALYSIS

Energy, Department of

BUDGETING (GOVERNMENTAL)

U.S. Marshals Service **(Justice)**

BUSINESS (GENERAL BUSINESS)

ACTION
Board of Governors of the Federal Reserve
System
Defense Logistics Agency **(Defense)**
Equal Employment Opportunity
Commission

Executive Office of the President
Export-Import Bank of the United States
Federal Highway Administration
(Transportation)
Federal Maritime Commission
Federal Railroad Administration
(Transportation)
Financial Management Service **(Treasury)**
Office of the Secretary **(Commerce)**
Patent and Trademark Office **(Commerce)**
U.S. Mint **(Treasury)**
Veterans Affairs, Department of

BUSINESS ADMINISTRATION

Agency for International Development
Agriculture, Department of
Agricultural Stabilization and
Conservation Service **(Agriculture)**
Army Corps of Engineers **(Defense)**
Army Finance and Accounting Center
(Defense)
Army Military District of Washington
(Defense)
Departmental Offices **(Treasury)**
Economic Affairs **(Commerce)**
Economic Development Administration
(Commerce)
Executive Office for U.S. Attorneys
(Justice)
Farm Credit Administration **(Agriculture)**
Federal Deposit Insurance Corporation
Federal Emergency Management Agency
Federal Railroad Administration
Federal Retirement Thrift Investment Board
Federal Trade Commission
General Accounting Office
General Services Administration
Government Printing Office
Health Care Financing Administration
(Health and Human Services)
Housing and Urban Development,
Department of
Interior, Department of
Internal Revenue Service **(Treasury)**
International Trade Administration
(Commerce)
International Trade Commission
Justice, Department Of ,

Maritime Administration (**Transportation**)
Minority Business Development Agency
  (**Commerce**)
National Labor Relations Board
National Park Service (**Interior**)
National Science Foundation
Office of the Comptroller of the Currency
  (**Treasury**)
Office of Inspector General
  (**Transportation**)
Office of Personnel Management
Office of Thrift Supervision (**Treasury**)
Research and Special Programs
  Administration (**Transportation**)
Rural Electrification Administration
  (**Agriculture**)
Savings Bonds Division (**Treasury**)
Selective Service System
Small Business Administration
State, Department of
Transportation, Department of
Travel and Tourism Administration
  (**Commerce**)
Urban Mass Transportation Administration
  (**Transportation**)
U.S. Coast Guard (**Transportation**)
U.S. Customs Service (**Treasury**)
U.S. Marshals Service (**Justice**)

BUSINESS LAW
U.S. Customs Service (**Treasury**)

BUSINESS MANAGEMENT
Food and Nutrition Service (**Agriculture**)
National Credit Union Administration
Navy (**Defense**)
Office of Inspector General
  (**Transportation**)

CARTOGRAPHY
Bureau of the Census (**Commerce**)
Bureau of Land Management (**Interior**)
Defense Mapping Agency (**Defense**)
National Oceanic and Atmospheric
  Administration (**Commerce**)
U.S. Customs Service (**Treasury**)

CERAMIC ENGINEERING
National Institute of Standards and
  Technology (**Commerce**)
Navy (**Defense**)

CHEMICAL ENGINEERING
Army Materiel Command (**Defense**)
Agricultural Research Service
  (**Agriculture**)
Drug Enforcement Administration (**Justice**)
Environmental Protection Agency
National Aeronautics and Space
  Administration
National Institute of Standards and
  Technology (**Commerce**)
Navy (**Defense**)
Nuclear Regulatory Commission
Patent and Trademark Office (**Commerce**)
Tennessee Valley Authority

CHEMISTRY
Animal and Plant Health Inspection
  Service (**Agriculture**)
Agricultural Research Service
  (**Agriculture**)
Bureau of Engraving and Printing
  (**Treasury**)
Drug Enforcement Administration (**Justice**)
Environmental Protection Agency
Federal Bureau of Investigation (**Justice**)
Food Safety and Inspection Service
  (**Agriculture**)
Government Printing Office
International Trade Commission
National Archives and Records
  Administration
National Institute of Standards and
  Technology (**Commerce**)
National Technical Information Service
  (**Commerce**)
Navy (**Defense**)
Patent and Trademark Office (**Commerce**)
Research and Special Programs
  Administration (**Transportation**)
U.S. Geological Survey (**Interior**)

CHINESE
Drug Enforcement Administration **(Justice)**

CIVIL ENGINEERING
Army Corps of Engineers **(Defense)**
Bureau of Reclamation **(Interior)**
Defense Mapping Agency **(Defense)**
Environmental Protection Agency
Farmers Home Administration
  (Agriculture)
Federal Aviation Administration
  (Transportation)
Federal Emergency Management Agency
Federal Highway Administration
  (Transportation)
Forest Service **(Agriculture)**
General Services Administration
National Institute of Standards and
  Technology **(Commerce)**
Navy **(Defense)**
State, Department of
Tennessee Valley Authority
Urban Mass Transportation Administration
  (Transportation)
U.S. Geological Survey **(Interior)**

CLINICAL PSYCHOLOGY
Bureau of Prisons **(Justice)**

COMMERCE
Navy **(Defense)**

COMMERCIAL LAW
Office of the Comptroller of the Currency
  (Treasury)

COMMUNICATIONS
Federal Retirement Thrift Investment Board
Labor, Department of
National Archives and Records
  Administration
National Park Service **(Interior)**
National Science Foundation
National Telecommunications and
  Information Administration
  (Commerce)
Small Business Administration

U.S. Information Agency
Voice of America **(U.S. Information
  Agency)**

COMMUNICATIONS (VISUAL)
Defense Mapping Agency **(Defense)**

COMMUNITY PLANNING
Economic Development Administration
  (Commerce)
Environmental Protection Agency
Housing and Urban Development,
  Department of

COMPARATIVE RELIGION
National Endowment for the Humanities

**COMPUTER AND
INFORMATION SYSTEMS**
Navy **(Defense)**

COMPUTER ENGINEERING
Federal Bureau of Investigation **(Justice)**
Navy **(Defense)**

COMPUTER SCIENCE
Administrative Office of the U.S. Courts
Agriculture, Department of
Agricultural Stabilization and
  Conservation Service **(Agriculture)**
Army Corps of Engineers **(Defense)**
Army Finance and Accounting Center
  (Defense)
Army Military District of Washington
  (Defense)
Board of Governors of the Federal Reserve
  System
Bureau of the Census **(Commerce)**
Bureau of Engraving and Printing
  (Treasury)
Bureau of Economic Analysis
  (Commerce)
Bureau of Export Administration
  (Commerce)
Bureau of Indian Affairs **(Interior)**
Bureau of Labor Statistics **(Labor)**
Bureau of Land Management **(Interior)**

Bureau of the Public Debt **(Treasury)**
Commodity Futures Trading Commission
Consumer Product Safety Commission
Defense Communications Agency
  (Defense)
Defense Intelligence Agency **(Defense)**
Defense Logistics Agency **(Defense)**
Defense Mapping Agency **(Defense)**
Departmental Offices **(Treasury)**
Drug Enforcement Administration **(Justice)**
Employment and Training Administration
  (Labor)
Energy, Department of
Executive Office for U.S. Attorneys
  (Justice)
Executive Office of the President
Export-Import Bank of the United States
Federal Bureau of Investigation **(Justice)**
Federal Emergency Management Agency
Federal Highway Administration
  (Transportation)
Federal Retirement Thrift Investment Board
Federal Trade Commission
Financial Management Service **(Treasury)**
General Accounting Office
General Services Administration
Government Printing Office
Health Care Financing Administration
  (Health and Human Services)
Housing and Urban Development,
  Department of
Immigration and Naturalization Service
  (Justice)
Internal Revenue Service **(Treasury)**
International Trade Commission
Justice, Department of
Labor, Department of
Library of Congress
Merit Systems Protection Board
National Aeronautics and Space
  Administration
National Institute of Standards and
  Technology **(Commerce)**
National Oceanic and Atmospheric
  Administration **(Commerce)**
National Security Agency **(Defense)**
National Technical Information Service
  (Commerce)

National Telecommunications and
  Information Administration
  (Commerce)
Navy **(Defense)**
Office of Justice Programs **(Justice)**
Office of the Secretary **(Commerce)**
Patent and Trademark Office **(Commerce)**
St. Lawrence Seaway Development
  Corporation **(Transportation)**
Securities and Exchange Commission
Selective Service System
Small Business Administration
Social Security Administration **(Health
  and Human Services)**
State, Department of
Tennessee Valley Authority
U.S. Customs Service **(Treasury)**
U.S. Marshals Service **(Justice)**
Veterans Affairs, Department of

CONSERVATION
Smithsonian Institution

CONTRACTING
Energy, Department of

CORRECTIONS
Secret Service **(Treasury)**

CORRECTIVE THERAPY
Veterans Affairs, Department of

COUNSELING PSYCHOLOGY
Veterans Affairs, Department of

CREATIVE ARTS THERAPY
Veterans Affairs, Department of

CREATIVE WRITING
Labor, Department of

CREDIT
Farm Credit Administration **(Agriculture)**
Small Business Administration

CRIMINAL INVESTIGATION
Housing and Urban Development,
Department of

**CRIMINAL JUSTICE
(CRIMINOLOGY)**
Bureau of Land Management **(Interior)**
Bureau of Prisons **(Justice)**
Departmental Offices **(Treasury)**
Drug Enforcement Administration **(Justice)**
Federal Emergency Management Agency
Federal Law Enforcement Training Center
(Treasury)
General Services Administration
Government Printing Office
Immigration and Naturalization Service
(Justice)
Interior, Department of the
Justice, Department of
Office of Inspector General **(Agriculture)**
(Health and Human Services)
(Transportation)
Railroad Retirement Board
Secret Service **(Treasury)**
U.S. Customs Service **(Treasury)**
U.S. Marshals Service **(Justice)**

CRYPTOGRAPHY
State, Department of

CRYPTOLOGY
Federal Bureau of Investigation **(Justice)**

CULTURAL ANTHROPOLOGY
U.S. Information Agency

CYTOTECHNOLOGY
Navy **(Defense)**

DATA MANAGEMENT
Financial Management Service **(Treasury)**

DATA PROCESSING
Defense Mapping Agency **(Defense)**
U.S. Marshals Service **(Justice)**

DENTAL HYGIENE
Navy **(Defense)**
Veterans Affairs, Department of

DENTISTRY
Bureau of Prisons**(Justice)**
Indian Health Service **(Health and
Human Services)**
National Institutes of Health **(Health and
Human Services)**

DIETETICS
Indian Health Service **(Health and
Human Services)**
Veterans Affairs, Department of

EARTH SCIENCE
Defense Intelligence Agency **(Defense)**
Defense Mapping Agency **(Defense)**

ECONOMICS
Agency for International Development
Army Finance and Accounting Center
(Defense)
Board of Governors of the Federal Reserve
System
Bureau of the Census **(Commerce)**
Bureau of Economic Analysis
(Commerce)
Bureau of Labor Statistics **(Labor)**
Bureau of Land Management **(Interior)**
Bureau of Mines **(Interior)**
Commission on Civil Rights
Commodity Futures Trading Commission
Defense Logistics Agency **(Defense)**
Departmental Offices**(Treasury)**
Drug Enforcement Administration **(Justice)**
Economic Affairs **(Commerce)**
Economics Management Staff
(Agriculture)
Employment and Training Administration
(Labor)
Environmental Protection Agency
Executive Office of the President
Export-Import Bank of the United States
Federal Deposit Insurance Corporation
Federal Maritime Commission

General Services Administration
International Trade Commission
Justice, Department of
National Institute of Standards and
Technology **(Commerce)**
National Telecommunications and
Information Administration
(Commerce)
Navy **(Defense)**
Rural Electrification Administration
(Agriculture)
State, Department of

ELECTRONICS TECHNOLOGY
Voice of America **(U.S. Information
Agency)**

ENGINEERING (GENERAL)
Bureau of Indian Affairs **(Interior)**
Bureau of Land Management **(Interior)**
Bureau of Mines **(Interior)**
Consumer Product Safety Commission
Defense Logistics Agency **(Defense)**
Defense Mapping Agency **(Defense)**
Drug Enforcement Administration **(Justice)**
Energy, Department of
Federal Communications Commission
Government Printing Office
Housing and Urban Development,
Department of
Internal Revenue Service **(Treasury)**
Library of Congress
Maritime Administration **(Transportation)**
Military Traffic Management Command
(Defense)
Minerals Management Service **(Interior)**
National Highway Traffic Safety
Administration **(Transportation)**
National Institute of Standards and
Technology **(Commerce)**
National Oceanic and Atmospheric
Administration **(Commerce)**
National Technical Information Service
(Commerce)
Navy **(Defense)**
Office of Surface Mining Reclamation and
Enforcement **(Interior)**
Patent and Trademark Office **(Commerce)**

Research and Special Programs
Administration **(Transportation)**
Smithsonian Institution
Soil Conservation Service **(Agriculture)**
State, Department of
Urban Mass Transportation Administration
(Transportation)
U.S. Coast Guard **(Transportation)**
U.S. Customs Service **(Treasury)**
Veterans Affairs, Department of

ENGINEERING MANAGEMENT
Navy **(Defense)**

ENGINEERING PSYCHOLOGY
Consumer Product Safety Commission

ENGINEERING TECHNOLOGY
Army Corps of Engineers **(Defense)**
Navy **(Defense)**

ENGLISH
Federal Trade Commission
Labor, Department of
National Archives and Records
Administration
Navy **(Defense)**
Research and Special Programs
Administration **(Transportation)**
U.S. Information Agency

ENTOMOLOGY
Animal and Plant Health Inspection
Service **(Agriculture)**
Forest Service **(Agriculture)**

ENVIRONMENTAL
ENGINEERING
Environmental Protection Agency
Navy **(Defense)**
Nuclear Regulatory Commission

ENVIRONMENTAL SCIENCE
(ENVIRONMENTAL STUDIES)
Bureau of Land Management **(Interior)**
Environmental Protection Agency

ETHICS
National Endowment for the Humanities

FILM AND DRAMA
U.S. Information Agency

FINANCE
Administrative Office of the U.S. Courts
Army Finance and Accounting Center
  (Defense)
Board of Governors of the Federal Reserve
  System
Defense Logistics Agency **(Defense)**
Departmental Offices **(Treasury)**
Economic Affairs **(Commerce)**
Export-Import Bank of the United States
Farm Credit Administration **(Agriculture)**
Federal Deposit Insurance Corporation
Federal Emergency Management Agency
Federal Retirement Thrift Investment Board
Financial Management Service **(Treasury)**
General Accounting Office
International Trade Administration
  (Commerce)
National Credit Union Administration
Office of the Comptroller of the Currency
  (Treasury)
Office of the Secretary **(Commerce)**
Office of Thrift Supervision **(Treasury)**
Rural Electrification Administration
  (Agriculture)
Securities and Exchange Commission
Small Business Administration
State, Department of
Travel and Tourism Administration
  (Commerce)
U.S. Postal Service

FINANCIAL MANAGEMENT
Economic Development Administration
  (Commerce)
Minority Business Development Agency
  (Commerce)
Navy **(Defense)**
St. Lawrence Seaway Development
  (Transportation)

FINE ARTS
Smithsonian Institution

FIRE PREVENTION ENGINEERING
National Institute of Standards and
  Technology **(Commerce)**

FIRE SCIENCE
Navy **(Defense)**

FISHERY BIOLOGY
Forest Service **(Agriculture)**
National Oceanic and Atmospheric
  Administration **(Commerce)**

FOOD ENGINEERING
Agricultural Research Service
  (Agriculture)

FOOD TECHNOLOGY (FOOD SCIENCE)
Agricultural Marketing Service
  (Agriculture)
Agricultural Research Service
  (Agriculture)
Food Safety and Inspection Service
  (Agriculture)

FOREIGN AFFAIRS (FOREIGN POLICY)
Bureau of Export Administration
  (Commerce)
U.S. Information Agency

FOREIGN AREA STUDIES
Defense Intelligence Agency **(Defense)**

FORESTRY
Bureau of Land Management **(Interior)**
Defense Mapping Agency **(Defense)**
Forest Service **(Agriculture)**
International Trade Commission
National Park Service **(Interior)**
U.S. Customs Service **(Treasury)**

GENERAL ADMINISTRATION
Energy, Department of
Navy **(Defense)**

GENETICS
Agricultural Research Service
 (Agriculture)

GEOCHEMICAL ENGINEERING
Nuclear Regulatory Commission

GEODESY
Defense Mapping Agency **(Defense)**
National Oceanic and Atmospheric
 Administration **(Commerce)**

GEOGRAPHY (GENERAL GEOGRAPHY, PHYSICAL GEOGRAPHY)
Bureau of the Census **(Commerce)**
Bureau of Land Management **(Interior)**
Defense Intelligence Agency **(Defense)**
Defense Mapping Agency **(Defense)**
Environmental Protection Agency
U.S. Customs Service **(Treasury)**
U.S. Information Agency

GEOLOGY (GEOLOGY SCIENCES)
Bureau of Land Management **(Interior)**
Bureau of Reclamation **(Interior)**
Defense Mapping Agency **(Defense)**
Environmental Protection Agency
Forest Service **(Agriculture)**
Minerals Management Service **(Interior)**
U.S. Customs Service **(Treasury)**
U.S. Geological Survey **(Interior)**

GEOPHYSICS
Defense Mapping Agency **(Defense)**
Minerals Management Service **(Interior)**

GEOPHYSIOLOGY
U.S. Geological Survey **(Interior)**

GOVERNMENT
National Archives and Records
 Administration
Navy **(Defense)**

HEALTH PHYSICS
Nuclear Regulatory Commission

HEALTH SCIENCES
Consumer Product Safety Commission

HEALTH SERVICES MANAGEMENT
Health Care Financing Administration
 (Health and Human Services)

HISTOPATHOLOGY
Navy **(Defense)**

HISTORY
Drug Enforcement Administration **(Justice)**
National Endowment for the Humanities
National Park Service **(Interior)**
Smithsonian Institution
U.S. Customs Service **(Treasury)**
U.S. Information Agency

HISTORY AND CRITICISM OF THE ARTS
National Endowment for the Humanities

HOME ECONOMICS
Food and Nutrition Service **(Agriculture)**

HORTICULTURE
Agricultural Marketing Service
 (Agriculture)

HOSPITAL ADMINISTRATION
Veterans Affairs, Department of

HYDROLOGY
Bureau of Land Management **(Interior)**
Bureau of Reclamation **(Interior)**
Environmental Protection Agency
Forest Service **(Agriculture)**

National Oceanic and Atmospheric
Administration **(Commerce)**
Office of Surface Mining
Reclamation and Enforcement **(Interior)**

**HYDROGEOLOGICAL
ENGINEERING
(GEOMORPHOLOGICAL,
GEOTECHNICAL)**
Nuclear Regulatory Commission

ILLUSTRATION
Veterans Affairs, Department of

INDUSTRIAL ARTS
State, Department of

INDUSTRIAL ECONOMICS
International Trade Administration
(Commerce)

INDUSTRIAL ENGINEERING
Bureau of Engraving and Printing
(Treasury)
Defense Mapping Agency **(Defense)**
International Trade Commission
National Aeronautics and Space
Administration
National Institute of Standards and
Technology **(Commerce)**
Navy **(Defense)**
Small Business Administration
U.S. Postal Service

INDUSTRIAL HYGIENE
Navy **(Defense)**
Occupational Safety and Health
Administration **(Labor)**

INDUSTRIAL MANAGEMENT
Navy **(Defense)**
Small Business Administration

INDUSTRIAL RELATIONS
Army Finance and Accounting Center
(Defense)

International Trade Administration
(Commerce)
National Labor Relations Board
Small Business Administration
U.S. Customs Service **(Treasury)**

INDUSTRIAL TECHNOLOGY
Defense Logistics Agency **(Defense)**

INFORMATION MANAGEMENT
Savings Bonds Division **(Treasury)**

INFORMATION SCIENCE
Library of Congress

INTERIOR DESIGN
Veterans Affairs, Department of

INTERNATIONAL BUSINESS
Bureau of Export Administration
(Commerce)
International Trade Administration
(Commerce),

INTERNATIONAL ECONOMICS
International Trade Administration
(Commerce)
International Trade Commission

**INTERNATIONAL RELATIONS
(INTERNATIONAL AFFAIRS)**
Bureau of Export Administration
(Commerce)
Library of Congress
U.S. Information Agency
Voice of America **(U.S. Information
Agency)**

INTERNATIONAL TRADE
Bureau of Export Administration
(Commerce)
International Trade Administration
(Commerce)

JURISPRUDENCE
National Endowment for the Humanities

JOURNALISM

Agriculture, Department of
Federal Trade Commission
Labor, Department of
National Archives and Records
    Administration
Navy **(Defense)**
Savings Bonds Division **(Treasury)**
Small Business Administration
U.S. Information Agency
Voice of America **(U.S. Information
    Agency)**

LABOR RELATIONS

National Labor Relations Board
Small Business Administration
U.S. Customs Service **(Treasury)**

LANDSCAPE ARCHITECTURE

Forest Service **(Agriculture)**

LAND SURVEYING

Bureau of Land Management **(Interior)**

LANGUAGE STUDIES

Voice of America **(U.S. Information
    Agency)**

LANGUAGES (GENERAL)

Drug Enforcement Administration **(Justice)**
National Endowment for the Humanities

LAW

Administrative Office of the U.S. Courts
Agency for International Development
Board of Governors of the Federal Reserve
    System
Bureau of Land Management **(Interior)**
Commission on Civil Rights
Commodity Futures Trading Commission
Drug Enforcement Administration **(Justice)**
Equal Employment Opportunity
    Commission
Executive Office of the President
Federal Aviation Administration
    (Transportation)
Federal Communications Commission

Federal Deposit Insurance Corporation
Federal Emergency Management Agency
Federal Maritime Commission
Federal Railroad Administration
    (Transportation)
Federal Retirement Thrift Investment Board
Federal Trade Commission
General Services Administration
Interior, Department of the
International Trade Commission
Labor, Department of
Library of Congress
Maritime Administration **(Transportation)**
Merit Systems Protection Board
National Highway Traffic Safety
    Administration **(Transportation)**
National Labor Relations Board
Navy **(Defense)**
Office of Attorney Personnel Management
    (Justice)
Office of the Secretary **(Commerce)**
    (Health andHuman Services)
Office of the Solicitor **(Labor)**
Office of Thrift Supervision **(Treasury)**
Patent and Trademark Office **(Commerce)**
Securities and Exchange Commission
Small Business Administration
State, Department of
Transportation, Department of
Commission on Civil Rights
U.S. Postal Service
Veterans Affairs, Department of

LAW ENFORCEMENT

Bureau of Export Administration
    (Commerce)
Bureau of Prisons **(Justice)**
Federal Law Enforcement Training Center
    (Treasury)
Justice, Department of
Navy **(Defense)**
Office of Inspector General **(Commerce)**
    (Health and Human Services) (Labor)
Secret Service **(Treasury)**
U.S. Customs Service **(Treasury)**

LIBERAL ARTS

Administrative Office of the U.S. Courts

Agriculture, Department of
Bureau of Indian Affairs **(Interior)**
Bureau of Land Management **(Interior)**
Consumer Product Safety Commission
Education, Department of
Federal Retirement Thrift Investment Board
General Services Administration
Health Care Financing Administration
  (Health and Human Services)
Interior, Department of the
Justice, Department of
National Highway Traffic Safety
  Administration **(Transportation)**
National Park Service **(Interior)**
National Science Foundation
Navy **(Defense)**
Office of the Secretary **(Commerce)**
Patent and Trademark Office **(Commerce)**
Research and Special Programs
  Administration **(Transportation)**
Savings Bonds Division **(Treasury)**
Transportation, Department of
U.S. Customs Service **(Treasury)**
U.S. Fish and Wildlife Service **(Interior)**

LIBRARY SCIENCE
Army Materiel Command **(Defense)**
Executive Office of the President
Government Printing Office
International Trade Commission
Library of Congress
National Technical Information Service
  (Commerce)
Navy **(Defense)**
Patent and Trademark Office **(Commerce)**
Smithsonian Institution
Veterans Affairs, Department of

LIFE SCIENCES
Drug Enforcement Administration **(Justice)**

LINGUISTICS
National Endowment for the Humanities

LITERATURE
Labor, Department of
National Endowment for the Humanities

LOGISTICS MANAGEMENT
Defense Mapping Agency **(Defense)**
Navy **(Defense)**
U.S. Customs Service **(Treasury)**

MANAGEMENT
Bureau of Export Administration
  (Commerce)
Economic Affairs **(Commerce)**
Federal Trade Commission
State, Department of

MANAGEMENT INFORMATION SYSTEMS
Board of Governors of the Federal Reserve
  System
Defense Intelligence Agency **(Defense)**
Defense Mapping Agency **(Defense)**
Financial Management Service **(Treasury)**
General Accounting Office
Health Care Financing Administration
  (Health and Human Services)
Office of Personnel Management
Office of Thrift Supervision **(Treasury)**

MANUAL ARTS THERAPY
Veterans Affairs, Department of

MARITIME STUDIES
Drug Enforcement Administration **(Justice)**

MARKETING
Bureau of Export Administration
  (Commerce)
Federal Deposit Insurance Corporation
Federal Retirement Thrift Investment Board
International Trade Administration
  (Commerce)
International Trade Commission
Minority Business Development Agency
  (Commerce)
National Technical Information Service
  (Commerce)
Navy **(Defense)**
Savings Bonds Division **(Treasury)**

Travel and Tourism Administration
(**Commerce**)
U.S. Mint (**Treasury**)

MATERIALS ENGINEERING
National Institute of Standards and
Technology (**Commerce**)
Navy (**Defense**)
Nuclear Regulatory Commission

MATHEMATICS
Army Military District of Washington
(**Defense**)
Bureau of Labor Statistics (**Labor**)
Defense Logistics Agency (**Defense**)
Defense Mapping Agency (**Defense**)
Drug Enforcement Administration (**Justice**)
Economics Management Staff
(**Agriculture**)
Employment and Training Administration
(**Labor**)
Health Care Financing Administration
(**Health and Human Services**)
Justice, Department of
Library of Congress
National Aeronautics and Space
Administration
National Highway Traffic Safety
Administration (**Transportation**)
National Institute of Standards and
Technology (**Commerce**)
National Oceanic and Atmospheric
Administration (**Commerce**)
National Security Agency
National Technical Information Service
(**Commerce**)
Navy (**Defense**)
U.S. Customs Service (**Treasury**)

MECHANICAL ENGINEERING
Army Corps of Engineers (**Defense**)
Army Materiel Command (**Defense**)
Bureau of Engraving and Printing
(**Treasury**)
Drug Enforcement Administration (**Justice**)
Energy, Department of
Federal Aviation Administration

General Services Administration
International Trade Commission
National Aeronautics and Space
Administration
National Institute of Standards and
Technology (**Commerce**)
Navy (**Defense**)
Nuclear Regulatory Commission
Patent and Trademark OfFice (**Commerce**)
Tennessee Valley Authority
U.S. Postal Service

**MEDICAL RECORDS
TECHNOLOGY**
Navy (**Defense**)

MEDICAL TECHNOLOGY
Navy (**Defense**)
Veterans Affairs, Department of

MEDICINE
Agency for Toxic Substances and Disease
Registry (**Health and Human Services**)
Alcohol, Drug Abuse and Mental Health
Administration (**Health and Human
Services**)
Bureau of Prisons (**Justice**)
Food and Drug Administration (**Health
and Human Services**)
Indian Health Service (**Health and
Human Services**)
National Institutes of Health (**Health and
Human Services**)
Navy (**Defense**)

METALLURGY
International Trade Commission
National Institute of Standards and
Technology (**Commerce**)
Navy (**Defense**)
Nuclear Regulatory Commission

METEOROLOGY
Defense Mapping Agency (**Defense**)
National Oceanic and Atmospheric
Administration (**Commerce**)

MICROBIAL GENETICS
Agricultural Research Service
(Agriculture)

MICROBIOLOGY
Animal and Plant Health Inspection
Service **(Agriculture)**
Agricultural Research Service
(Agriculture)
Food Safety and Inspection Service
(Agriculture)
Navy **(Defense)**
Patent and Trademark Office **(Commerce)**
Veterans Affairs, Department of

MILITARY SCIENCE
Drug Enforcement Administration **(Justice)**
Federal Emergency Management Agency
Navy **(Defense)**
U.S. Customs Service **(Treasury)**

MINERAL ECONOMICS
International Trade Commission

MOLECULAR BIOLOGY
Agricultural Research Service
(Agriculture)

**NATURAL RESOURCE
MANAGEMENT**
Army Corps of Engineers **(Defense)**

NAUTICAL SCIENCE
Defense Mapping Agency **(Defense)**

NAVAL ARCHITECTURE
Maritime Administration **(Transportation)**

NAVAL ENGINEERING
Navy **(Defense)**

NAVIGATION
Defense Mapping Agency **(Defense)**

NEAR EASTERN LANGUAGES
National Security Agency

NUCLEAR ENGINEERING
Energy, Department of
Navy **(Defense)**
Nuclear Regulatory Commission
Tennessee Valley Authority

**NURSING (PRACTICAL,
VOCATIONAL)**
Navy **(Defense)**

NURSING (PROFESSIONAL)
Bureau of Prisons **(Justice)**
Government Printing Office
Indian Health Service **(Health and
Human Services)**
National Institutes of Health **(Health and
Human Services)**
Navy **(Defense)**
Veterans Affairs, Department of

NUTRITION
Food and Nutrition Service **(Agriculture)**
Veterans Affairs, Department of

**OCCUPATIONAL HEALTH
MANAGEMENT**
Navy **(Defense)**

OCCUPATIONAL THERAPY
Veterans Affairs, Department of

OCEAN ENGINEERING
Navy **(Defense)**

**OCEANOGRAPHY (GENERAL,
GEOLOGICAL, PHYSICAL)**
Defense Mapping Agency **(Defense)**
National Oceanic and Atmospheric
Administration **(Commerce)**
Navy **(Defense)**

OPERATIONS RESEARCH
Energy, Department of

ORTHOTICS
Veterans Affairs, Department of

PAPER CONSERVATION
National Archives and Records
Administration

PARALEGAL STUDIES
Executive Office for U.S. Attorneys
(**Justice**)
Federal Trade Commission
Justice, Department of

**PARK AND RECREATION
MANAGEMENT**
Army Corps of Engineers

**PERSONNEL (HUMAN
RESOURCES MANAGEMENT,
PERSONNEL
ADMINISTRATION,
PERSONNEL MANAGEMENT)**
Army Finance and Accounting Center
(**Justice**)
Financial Management Service (**Treasury**)
National Labor Relations Board
Navy (**Defense**)
Office of Personnel Management
Small Business Administration
U.S. Customs Service (**Treasury**)
U.S. Marshals Service (**Justice**)

PHARMACOLOGY
Drug Enforcement Administration (**Justice**)
Environmental Protection Agency

PHARMACY
Drug Enforcement Administration (**Justice**)
Navy (**Defense**)
Veterans Affairs, Department of

PHILOSOPHY
National Endowment for the Humanities

PHOTO GRAMMETRY
Defense Mapping Agency (**Defense**)

PHOTO INTERPRETATION
Defense Mapping Agency (**Defense**)

PHOTOGRAPHY
Drug Enforcement Administration (**Justice**)
Federal Bureau of Investigation (**Justice**)

PHYSICAL EDUCATION
Veterans Affairs, Department of

PHYSICAL SCIENCES
Bureau of Land Management (**Interior**)
Bureau of Mines (**Interior**)
Bureau of Reclamation (**Interior**)
Defense Logistics Agency (**Defense**)
Drug Enforcement Administration (**Justice**)
Environmental Protection Agency
Library of Congress
National Institute of Standards and
Technology (**Commerce**)
National Park Service (**Interior**)
Navy (**Defense**)
U.S. Customs Service (**Treasury**)
U.S. Geological Survey (**Interior**)

PHYSICAL THERAPY
Veterans Affairs, Department of

PHYSICS
Defense Mapping Agency (**Defense**)
Federal Bureau of Investigation (**Justice**)
National Aeronautics and Space
Administration
National Archives and Records
Administration
National Institute of Standards and
Technology (**Commerce**)
National Oceanic and Atmospheric
Administration (**Commerce**)
Navy (**Defense**)
Patent and Trademark Office (**Commerce**)
State, Department of

PLANT PATHOLOGY
Animal and Plant Health Inspection
Service (**Agriculture**)
Forest Service (**Agriculture**)

PLANT PHYSIOLOGY
Agricultural Research Service
 (Agriculture)

POLICE SCIENCE (POLICE ADMINISTRATION)
Federal Law Enforcement Training Center
 (Treasury)
Navy **(Defense)**
U.S. Customs Service **(Treasury)**
U.S. Marshals Service **(Justice)**

POLISH
Federal Bureau of Investigation **(Justice)**

POLITICAL SCIENCE
Agriculture, Department of
Defense Logistics Agency **(Defense)**
Drug Enforcement Administration **(Justice)**
Education, Department of
Environmental Protection Agency
Federal Trade Commission
General Accounting Office
Justice, Department of
Library of Congress .
National Archives and Records
 Administration
National Labor Relations Board
Navy **(Defense)**
Small Business Administration
U.S. Customs Service **(Treasury)**
U.S. Information Agency

PORTUGUESE
Drug Enforcement Agency **(Justice)**

POULTRY SCIENCE
Agricultural Marketing Service
 (Agriculture)

PRINTING MANAGEMENT
Government Printing Office

PROCUREMENT
Financial Management Service **(Treasury)**

PRODUCTION MANAGEMENT
Navy **(Defense)**

PSYCHIATRY
Bureau of Prisons **(Justice)**

PROGRAM ANALYSIS
Energy, Department of

PROSTHETICS
Veterans Affairs, Department of

PSYCHOLOGY
Alcohol, Drug Abuse and Mental Health
 Administration **(Health and Human
 Services)**
Army Finance and Accounting Center
 (Defense)
Navy **(Defense)**
Small Business Administration
U.S. Customs Service **(Treasury)**
U.S. Postal Service
Veterans Affairs, Department of

PUBLIC ADMINISTRATION
Army Finance and Accounting Center
 (Defense)
Bureau of Export Administration
 (Commerce)
Defense Logistics Agency **(Defense)**
Environmental Protection Agency
Executive Office of the President
Federal Emergency Management Agency
Federal Trade Commission
General Accounting Office
General Services Administration
Health Care Financing Administration
 (Health and Human Services)
Housing and Urban Development,
 Department of
National Labor Relations Board
National Science Foundation
Navy **(Defense)**
Office of Inspector General
 (Transportation)
Office of Personnel Management

Research and Special Programs
   Administration **(Transportation)**
Selective Service System
Small Business Administration
Transportation, Department of
Urban Mass Transportation Administration
   (Transportation)
U.S. Customs Service **(Treasury)**
U.S. Marshals Service **(Justice)**

PUBLIC AFFAIRS.
Agriculture, Department of

PUBLIC HEALTH
Health Care Financing Administration
   (Health and Human Services)
U.S. Customs Service **(Treasury)**

PUBLIC POLICY
Executive Office of the President
Library of Congress
Minority Business Development Agency
   (Commerce)

PUSHTU
Drug Enforcement Administration **(Justice)**

PUBLIC UTILITIES
Energy, Department of

PURCHASING
Navy **(Defense)**

RADIO AND TELEVISION
Voice of America **(U.S. Information
   Agency)**

RADIO TELEPHONY
State, Department of

RANGE CONSERVATION
(RANGE MANAGEMENT)
Forest Service **(Agriculture)**
Soil Conservation Service **(Agriculture)**

RECREATION THERAPY
Veterans Affairs, Department of

REMOTE SENSING
Defense Intelligence Agency **(Defense)**
Defense Mapping Agency **(Defense)**

RESPIRATORY THERAPY
Navy **(Defense)**
Veterans Affairs, Department of

RUSSIAN
Federal Bureau of Investigation **(Justice)**

SAFETY ENGINEERING
Navy **(Defense)**

SCIENCE (ANY SCIENCE,
GENERAL SCIENCE)
Agency for Toxic Substances and Disease
   Registry **(Health and Human Services)**
Agriculture, Department of
Centers for Disease Control **(Health and
   Human Services)**
Food and Drug Administration **(Health
   and Human Services)**
Minerals Management Service **(Interior)**
National Institutes of Health **(Health and
   Human Services)**
National Science Foundation
Smithsonian Institution
State, Department of

SECRETARIAL STUDIES
(SECRETARIAL SCIENCE)
Federal Emergency Management Agency
Federal Trade Commission
Navy **(Defense)**

SECURITY ADMINISTRATION
Defense Mapping Agency **(Defense)**
Energy, Department of

SLAVIC LANGUAGES
National Security Agency **(Defense)**

SOCIAL SCIENCE
Commission on Civil Rights
Employment and Training Administration
(**Labor**)
General Accounting Office
Health Care Financing Administration
(**Health and Human Services**)
Library of Congress
National Endowment for the Humanities
Office of Human Development Services
(**Health and Human Services**)
Office of Justice Programs (**Justice**)

SOCIAL WORK
Alcohol, Drug Abuse and Mental Health
Administration (**Health and Human
Services**)
Bureau of Indian Affairs (**Interior**)
Bureau of Prisons (**Justice**)
Navy (**Defense**)
Veterans Affairs, Department of

SOCIOLOGY
Agriculture, Department of
Alcohol, Drug Abuse and Mental Health
Administration (**Health and Human
Services**)
Drug Enforcement Administration (**Justice**)
Environmental Protection Agency
U.S. Customs Service (**Treasury**)
U.S. Information Agency

SOIL SCIENCE (SOIL
CONSERVATION)
Defense Mapping Agency (**Defense**)
Forest Service (**Agriculture**)
Soil Conservation Service (**Agriculture**)

SPACE SCIENCE
Navy (**Defense**)

SPANISH
Drug Enforcement Administration (**Justice**)
Federal Bureau of Investigation (**Justice**)

SPEECH PATHOLOGY
Veterans Affairs, Department of

STATISTICS
Army Military District of Washington
(**Defense**)
Bureau of the Census (**Commerce**)
Bureau of Economic Analysis
(**Commerce**)
Bureau of Labor Statistics (**Labor**)
Commission on Civil Rights
Defense Logistics Agency (**Defense**)
Economics Management Staff
(**Agriculture**)
Executive Office of the President
Office of Justice Programs (**Justice**)
Travel and Tourism Administration
(**Commerce**)
U.S. Customs Service (**Treasury**)
Veterans Affairs, Department of

SYSTEMS MANAGEMENT
State, Department of

SURVEYING
Defense Mapping Agency (**Defense**)

TECHNICAL WRITING
Navy (**Defense**)

TELECOMMUNICATIONS
U.S. Customs Service (**Treasury**)

TEXTILE TECHNOLOGY
International Trade Commission

TOXICOLOGY
Drug Enforcement Administration (**Justice**)

TRANSPORTATION
Military Traffic Management Command
(**Defense**)
Urban Mass Transportation Administration
(**Transportation**)

TRANSPORTATION
ENGINEERING
Federal Highway Administration
(**Transportation**)

TV PRODUCTION
U.S. Information Agency

URBAN PLANNING
Federal Emergency Management Agency

URDU
Drug Enforcement Administration **(Justice)**

VETERINARY MEDICINE
Food and Drug Administration **(Health and Human Services)**

Food Safety and Inspection Service **(Agriculture)**

VETERINARY SCIENCE
Animal and Plant Health Inspection Service **(Agriculture)**

WILDLIFE BIOLOGY
Forest Service **(Agriculture)**